Church-State Constitutional Issues

Recent Titles in
Contributions in Legal Studies

John Marshall's Achievement: Law, Politics, and Constitutional Interpretations
Thomas C. Shevory, editor

Affirmative Action and Principles of Justice
Kathanne W. Greene

Unfounded Fears: Myths and Realities of a Constitutional Convention
Paul J. Weber and Barbara Perry

Protecting Constitutional Freedoms: A Role for Federal Courts
Daan Braveman

The Employment Relationship in Anglo-American Law: A Historical Perspective
Marc Linder

The Aristrocracy of the Long Robe
J. M. Sosin

Equal Separation: Understanding the Religion Clauses of the First Amendment
Paul J. Weber, editor

Common Law in Southern Africa: Conflict of Laws and Torts Precedents
Peter B. Kutner

A History of the Anglo-American Common Law of Contract
Kevin M. Teeven

"We Have a Duty": The Supreme Court and the Watergate Tapes Litigation
Howard Ball

The Shaping of Nineteenth-Century Law: John Appleton and Responsible Individualism
David M. Gold

Comparative Constitutional Federalism: Europe and America
Mark Tushnet, editor

CHURCH-STATE CONSTITUTIONAL ISSUES

Making Sense of the Establishment Clause

Donald L. Drakeman

Contributions in Legal Studies, Number 62
Paul L. Murphy, Series Editor

GREENWOOD PRESS
New York • Westport, Connecticut • London

Library of Congress Cataloging-in-Publication Data

Drakeman, Donald L.
Church-state constitutional issues : making sense of the establishment clause / Donald L. Drakeman.
p. cm. — (Contributions in legal studies, ISSN 0147–1074; no. 62)
Includes bibliographical references and index.
ISBN 0–313–27663–3 (alk. paper)
1. Church and state—United States—History. 2. United States—Constitutional history. 3. Established churches—United States—History. I. Title. II. Series.
KF4865.D73 1991
342.73'0852—dc20
[347.302852] 90–45464

British Library Cataloguing in Publication Data is available.

Library of Congress Catalog Card Number: 90–45464
ISBN: 0–313–27663–3
ISSN: 0147–1074

First published in 1991

Greenwood Press, 88 Post Road West, Westport, CT 06881
An imprint of Greenwood Publishing Group, Inc.

Printed in the United States of America

The paper used in this book complies with the Permanent Paper Standard issued by the National Information Standards Organization (Z39.48–1984).

10 9 8 7 6 5 4 3 2 1

CONTENTS

PREFACE

> "On your knees, America!"
>
> No, too forceful, concluded the President's writer. How about, "In God We Trust" has been a watchword for Americans since our forefathers . . . ?
>
> Wrong again, Timothy Burnham thought: Too wordy, too mealy-mouthed, too avuncular. . . . If the President wants the citizens to pray, he should tell them to pray.[1]

Unfortunately, novelist Peter Benchley quickly involves Burnham in international intrigue, thus preventing us from finding out how the thoughtful speechwriter would have penned the presidential proclamation declaring a National Day of Prayer. We must instead go to the *Federal Register*, which duly records all such presidential statements, although we should keep in mind the force of these pronouncements. As Timothy Burnham says on behalf of Benchley, himself a former presidential speechwriter, "Why bother with proclamations? Nobody ever reads them, let alone heeds them. The newspapers print them between the obituaries and the neuter-your-pet notices."[2]

Heeded or not, presidential prayer proclamations have become an annual ritual, and for the purpose of setting aside May 5, 1988, as the day for "all Americans to pray, each after his or her own manner, for unity in the hearts of all mankind," President Reagan's real speechwriters chose the mealymouthed approach: "Americans in every generation have turned to their Maker in prayer."[3] Several hundred words later, however, the tone changes from statements of historical fact to proclamations of national faith evoking the ringing cadences of the revivalists: "Let us [pray] for the love of God and His great goodness, in search of His guidance and the grace of repentance, in seeking His blessings, His peace, and the resting of His kind and holy hands on ourselves, our Nation, our friends in the defense of freedom, and all mankind, now and always."[4]

This is pretty strong language from the president of a country in which the separation of church and state is a central tenet of the national creed. Even fictional Timothy Burnham had the presence of mind to worry about "that piece of parchment called the Constitution." As far as he was concerned, "It's none of the President's business who prays when, how or to whom. The law says he has to keep his sticky fingers off religion."[5] And so it does, in the First Amendment to the Constitution. Yet at the same time, generations of Americans, from the days of the Puritans to the present, have proclaimed that God and country are joined together in pursuit of this nation's special role in world history. We are thus a nation pursuing with equal vigor a commitment to both a divine destiny and a complete separation of church and state. It is small wonder, then, that the relationship of religion to the republic over the last two centuries has been difficult and complex.

For this and a multitude of other reasons, studying the relationship between church and state is fascinating. Not only do church-state issues regularly receive front-page coverage in the national news media, but they are the focus of scholarly inquiry in a number of disciplines, including law, religious studies, history, and political science. Each field brings its distinct perspective to bear on church-state questions, and while there is inevitably some cross-fertilization, several relatively independent bodies of literature have developed. Lawyers tend to ask how to interpret the law in particular cases, church historians focus on the interaction of governmental and ecclesiastical institutions, and so on. Even libraries have realized this methodological pluralism, shelving books on church-state issues in three or four different places under a variety of call numbers.

To some extent, the church-state literature can be visually represented as an unfinished bicycle wheel. At the hub are all of the facts and circumstances surrounding the relationship of religions and governments. Radiating out from the hub in several directions are spokes, one for each of the scholarly disciplines dealing with church-state issues. Frequently missing, however, is the outer rim—the part needed to smooth out the bumpy ride inevitably created by a handful of spokes working independently. I would like to say that my goal is to complete the circle in church-state studies by drawing together all of the rich resources developed over the centuries in several scholarly fields. Thus completed, the wheel could roll more smoothly and quickly for all who are concerned with this complicated subject. Such wheel making is, unfortunately, beyond the scope of my abilities, let alone this work on the establishment clause. Nevertheless, as someone who has, at one time or another, practiced law, studied religion and history, and taught political science, I feel inclined towards an interdisciplinary approach.

My focus is on the establishment clause of the First Amendment to the Constitution, and my question is one typically posed by lawyers and political scientists but frequently answered with appeals to history—What does the establishment clause mean? Since the Supreme Court is the final arbiter of constitutional questions, I will begin by tracing the Court's interpretation of the establishment clause from its early nineteenth-century decisions through the most recent cases. This discussion will show how heavily the Court has relied on both the historical background to the establishment clause and the changing role of religion in American culture. Then, to evaluate the Court's interpretive positions, I will look at the origins of the First Amendment as well as the evolving relationship of religion and government as it has been manifested in the courts. Finally, I intend to return to the original question by drawing both on this complex historical and cultural background and on the theories of constitutional interpretation developed by lawyers and political scientists to suggest a new approach to the establishment clause.

One stylistic note: Teachers of good writing often urge writers to avoid quotations. I have chosen to ignore this advice, especially in my discussion of Supreme Court cases. For lawyers, Supreme Court opinions are the Mishna to the Constitution's Torah. Over the last 200 years, the skeleton of the Constitution has necessarily taken its flesh from the Court's dictums, and lawyers hang on every available word.

I owe many thanks to a large group of people who contributed to this project. In particular, I want to mention Robert Alley, Horton M. Davies, Edward M. Gaffney, Jr., Anne Larsen, Terry Nystrom, Albert J. Raboteau, Robert P. Seawright, Lori J. Smith, and John F. Wilson, as well as my parents, who supported my education over almost three decades, Cindy and Amy Drakeman, whose thirst for ever more knowledge serves as a model for any scholarly inquiry, and especially Lisa Drakeman, whose love of learning and demanding standards of scholarship have inspired me throughout this work.

NOTES

1. Peter Benchley, *Q Clearance* (New York: Random House, 1986), p. 3.
2. Ibid.
3. *Federal Register*, vol. 53, no. 24 (February 5, 1988).
4. Ibid.
5. Benchley, *Q*, p. 3.

1

THE SUPREME COURT AND THE ESTABLISHMENT CLAUSE

THE CONTEXT OF INTERPRETATION

When " 'I use a word,' Humpty Dumpty said, in a rather scornful tone, 'it means just what I choose it to mean—neither more nor less.' "[1] For one select group, the United States Supreme Court, Humpty Dumpty's aphorism is more than idle chatter. The Court seized final authority over the meaning of the Constitution in *Marbury v. Madison* (1803), announcing that "[i]t is emphatically the province and duty of the judicial department to say what the law is."[2] Since then, the nine justices of the Supreme Court have set the terms for constitutional debate. With or without the help of all the modern aids to textual criticism and interpretation—from dictionaries to deconstructionism—the Constitution means exactly what the Supreme Court chooses it to mean, neither more nor less. And so, when Alice asks Humpty Dumpty "whether you *can* make words mean so many different things," he responds as the Supreme Court did in *Marbury*, "The question is, . . . which is to be master—that's all."[3]

Textual interpretation is a task that the Court shares with many groups, but the closest analogy may be the way teachers and preachers try to elicit meaning from sacred writings. The Constitution has had almost as many exegetes as the Holy Scriptures, and the process of interpretation is remarkably similar. In each case, the document is seen as inspired, the author is unavailable for comment, and the limits of language make the interpretive process essential. As James Madison wrote in defense of the inevitably imperfect Constitution, "When the Almighty himself condescends to address mankind in their own language, his meaning, luminous as it must be, is rendered dim and doubtful by the cloudy medium through which it is communicated."[4] There is, however, one major difference in the interpretation of Scripture and the Constitution. Theologians taking their scriptural cases up to the Heavenly Council for final appeal are usually unable to share the outcome with us. Not so in the law, where almost every constitutional controversy reaching the Supreme Court provides the opportunity for the public ritual of interpretation: First, the parties make written and oral petitions to the Court; then the justices retire for secret discussions; finally, after the public invocation of God's blessing, the nine black-robed justices proceed into the High Court to render their interpretation of the Constitution's mandates.[5]

The Supreme Court has employed a variety of tools in this process of constitutional interpretation. It has frequently used the acts and statements of the "Founding Fathers" to shed light on what the Constitution's words meant to the men who enacted them. And the Court has also looked at a variety of political and cultural factors, the "plain meaning" of the words, the rules of grammar, preconstitutional law and a number of other lexical aids.

Constitutional interpretation is complicated by changes in circumstances over the two centuries since 1787, when the Constitution was adopted. Nowhere is this more clear than in the Court's struggles with the establishment clause of the First Amendment to the Constitution. The establishment clause, together with the free exercise clause, reads: "*Congress shall make no law respecting an establishment of religion* or prohibiting the free exercise thereof" (emphasis added). These religion clauses were adopted by the First Congress of the United States in 1789, and ratified by the states shortly thereafter; but the establishment clause was not discussed at length by the Supreme Court until 1947. In the intervening 160 years, the place of religion and religious institutions in American culture changed dramatically. Yet the Supreme Court justices have consistently relied heavily on their reading of the First Amendment's eighteenth-century historical and cultural backdrop to determine its meaning. We must ask, therefore, not only what the Founding Fathers intended but whether their eighteenth-century perceptions of what an establishment of religion meant should hold sway in light of twentieth-century church-state problems. And, ultimately, we must answer the question that, in the Supreme Court's hands, may have a significant effect on American religion and law in the years to come: What do the words "respecting an establishment of religion" mean in the context of the first amendment?

THE PROCESS OF INTERPRETATION

The Supreme Court's first significant case dealing with the religion clauses of the First Amendment was *Reynolds v. United States* (1879).[6]

George Reynolds, a member of the Mormon church and private secretary to Brigham Young, had been indicted under a federal statute providing a fine of $500 and imprisonment for up to five years for those found guilty of bigamy. One of Reynolds's defenses was that his church required men to practice polygamy and his refusal to do so would bring about his eternal damnation. The court had to decide whether the free exercise clause of the First Amendment would forbid Reynolds's conviction under the bigamy legislation. In reaching its decision to uphold both the law and Mr. Reynolds's indictment, the Supreme Court discussed at length the meaning of the word "religion" in the First Amendment, thus setting the stage for subsequent establishment clause cases.

Since there is no definition of the word "religion," the court said, "We must go elsewhere . . . to ascertain its meaning, and nowhere more appropriately, we think, than to the history of the times in the midst of which the provision was adopted."[7] The Court first reviewed the laws that had been enacted before the adoption of the Constitution providing public support for religion and for the punishment of various types of "heretical opinions." According to the Court, the "controversy upon this general subject was animated in many of the States, but seemed at last to culminate in Virginia."[8] The Virginia dispute involved a bill proposed in 1784 to provide an assessment to support teachers of the Christian religion. In opposition to this bill, James Madison prepared his famous "Memorial and Remonstrance" in which, according to the Court, "He demonstrated 'that religion, or the duty we owe the Creator,' was not within the cognizance of civil government."[9] After defeating the 1784 bill, the legislature enacted the bill for establishing religious freedom drafted by Thomas Jefferson. The Court then quoted from Jefferson's bill, observing that to permit the magistrate "to intrude his powers into the field of opinion, and to restrain the profession or propagation of principles on supposition of their ill tendency is a dangerous fallacy which at once destroys all religious liberty."[10] Yet even Jefferson conceived that this liberty could be constrained, for, in his words, "there is time enough for the rightful purposes of civil government for its officers to interfere when principles break out to overt acts against peace and good order."[11] In these statements by James Madison and Thomas Jefferson, the Court declared, "is found the true distinction between what properly belongs to the Church and what to the State."[12]

The Court then proceeded to review the history of the adoption of the First Amendment's religion clauses, beginning with Jefferson's disappointment that the draft Constitution had no declaration of religious freedom. Noting that several states in ratifying the Constitution had proposed amendments providing for religious freedom, the Court observed that the First Congress responded by adopting the First Amendment, which, the Supreme Court declared, was drafted by James Madison (an important historical issue to which we will return in the next chapter). The Court then quoted at length from Thomas Jefferson's letter to the Danbury Baptist Association, thus giving birth to one of the most troublesome judicial glosses in constitutional jurisprudence: "I contemplate with sovereign reverence that act of the whole American people which declared that their Legislature should 'Make no law respecting an establishment of religion or prohibiting the free exercise thereof,' thus building a wall of separation between Church and State."[13] According to Chief Justice Waite's majority opinion, Jefferson's letter "[c]oming as this does from an acknowledged leader of the advocates of the measure . . . may be accepted almost as an authoritative declaration of the scope and effect of the amendment thus secured."[14] Justice Waite failed to point out, however, that this "acknowledged leader" was not a member of the First Congress and was, in fact, in Europe when the First Amendment was adopted. And on this dubious historical reconstruction, numerous Supreme Court justices as well as politicians and even religious leaders have waxed eloquent about the American "wall of separation" between church and state.

Turning to the crime of polygamy and its treatment in Anglo-American law, the chief justice observed that Virginia had enacted a statute providing the death penalty for bigamy *after* it had passed the act establishing religious freedom. And so, since polygamy had never been tolerated in the United States, even in Virginia, the Court concluded that "it is impossible to believe that the constitutional guaranty of religious freedom was intended to prohibit legislation in respect to this most important feature of social life."[15] Although the free exercise clause prohibited Congress from interfering with religious beliefs, the Court saw nothing in the Constitution restricting the government's ability to regulate actions contrary to the public interest. This distinction between belief and action has proved a nettlesome one in free exercise cases, but for our establishment clause concerns, the importance of *Reynolds* lies in the Court's heavy reliance on Madison and Jefferson in its search for the meaning of the religion clauses of the First Amendment.

Almost one hundred years after its enactment, the establishment clause first surfaced in a Supreme Court case. This suit, *Davis v. Beason* (1890), also involved the indictment of a member of the Mormon church under a polygamy statute.[16] This time the defendant was not a practicing polygamist; he was convicted of falsely taking an oath (required of voters) that he was not a member of an organization advocating polygamy. After reviewing the religious freedom argument discussed in *Reynolds*, the Court reached the argument of counsel that "because no mode of worship can be established or religious tenets enforced in this country, therefore any form of worship may be followed and any tenets, however destructive of society, may be held and advocated, if asserted to be a part of the religious doctrines of those advocating and furthering them."[17] The Court refused to accept this aggressive reading of the establishment clause. Rather, it argued, "Whilst legislation for the establishment of religion is forbidden, and its free exercise permitted, it does not follow that everything that may be so called can be tolerated."[18] Thus, with little fanfare, the establishment clause made its debut in Supreme Court jurisprudence.

Reynolds and *Davis v. Beason* provide a brief case study of the Supreme Court's hand in the course of American religious history. Brigham Young had declared polygamy to be a tenet of the Mormon church in 1852, based upon an earlier revelation of the Prophet, Joseph Smith. Strong public sentiment in opposition led Congress to outlaw polygamy in the Territories, and several prominent churchmen were indicted, including George Reynolds and Brigham Young. The Reynolds case showed that the Supreme Court would stand behind the government's efforts to stamp out this practice. Then *Davis v. Beason*, involving a nonpolygamist who merely belonged to the Mormon church, demonstrated the long reach of the government's ability to prosecute. Finally, in *Church of Jesus Christ of Latter-Day Saints v. United States* (1890), the Court upheld a federal law revoking the Mormon church's charter and confiscating much of its property.[19] Faced with public antipathy, the potential of widespread criminal prosecutions, and the forfeiture of the church's property, the president of the Mormon church issued a proclamation saying that polygamous marriages were no longer sanctioned. This proclamation came only a few months after the decisions in *Davis v. Beason* and *Church of Jesus Christ of Latter-Day Saints v. United States*. Ultimately, there was a grant of amnesty and presidential pardon for all who abstained from polygamy after the proclamation.[20]

The Supreme Court's next establishment clause case came in 1899 in *Bradfield v. Roberts*.[21] Mr. Bradfield sought to enjoin the United States from paying any monies in support of the Providence Hospital in Washington, D.C. He argued that the hospital was owned and operated by the "Sisters of Charity of Emmitsburg, Maryland," a "Monastic Order" of the Roman Catholic church. To allow federal funds to go to this hospital, in Bradfield's view, would not only violate the establishment clause but would also provide a "precedent for giving to religious societies a legal agency in carrying into effect a public and civil duty which would, if once established, speedily obliterate the essential distinction between civil and religious functions."[22] The Court, however, concluded that Bradfield had no cause of action. Even assuming, "for the purpose of this question only," that federal support of a religious corporation operating a hospital would be an unconstitutional establishment of religion, there was no violation because the Providence Hospital was not a religious corporation. It was incorporated for the care of the sick in Washington and its certificate of incorporation said nothing about religion. Moreover, the federal legislation funding the hospital did not mention religion. Therefore, there could be no violation of the establishment clause. The religious beliefs or affiliations of the directors and officers of the corporation were irrelevant. As the Court stated, "[This] is simply the case of a secular corporation being managed by people who hold to the doctrines of the Roman Catholic Church, but who nevertheless are managing the corporation according to the [secular] law under which it exists."[23] The Court gave no further explanation of its interpretation of the establishment clause.

A decade later the Supreme Court heard the case of *Reuben Quick Bear v. Francis E. Leupp* (1908)[24] involving a dispute over the use of trust funds administered by the United States on behalf of American Indians as "the price of land ceded by the Indians to the Government."[25] Rueben Quick Bear, Ralph Eagle Feather, and several other members of the Sioux Tribe in South Dakota contested a proposed expenditure of the trust funds by the commissioner of Indian affairs. The funds were to go to the Bureau of Catholic Indian Missions for the education of a number of Indian children at a mission boarding school. A discussion of the establishment clause came almost as an afterthought. "Some reference is made to the Constitution, in respect to this contract with the Bureau of Indian Missions. It is not contended that it is unconstitutional, and it could not be [citing *Bradfield v. Roberts*]."[26] The plaintiffs then contended that the "spirit of the Constitution" required that no federal funds be appropriated for use in sectarian schools, especially since there was a statutory requirement to such effect applying to some of the funds held for the Indians. The Court decided that the trust funds were merely held for the benefit of the Indians who should be entitled to choose secular or sectarian education for their children. To refuse to allow the funds to be used for the Indian children to attend Catholic school would be to prohibit their free exercise of religion.[27]

Forty years passed before the Court turned again to the establishment clause, and, thus, it was not until 1947 that the Supreme Court gave the establishment clause more than a passing reference. In *Everson v. Board of Education* (1947), the Supreme Court was asked whether it was constitutional for the state of New Jersey to reimburse parents for money spent to transport their children to school by means of the public bus system.[28] Some of the state funds were used to reimburse parents of children attending Roman Catholic parochial schools. The statute was, therefore, challenged on the grounds that the state's support of the Catholic schools in this way was an unconstitutional establishment of religion. This is the first case asking the Court to invalidate a state action under the establishment clause since it decided in *Cantwell v. Connecticut* (1940) that the First Amendment's religion clauses apply to the states as well as to Congress (an issue to which we must return later).[29]

In *Everson*, Justice Black's majority opinion first briefly reviewed the history of religious freedom (and lack thereof) in America. The persecution of Quakers, Catholics, and Baptists, combined with the imposition of taxes to support certain churches "shock[ed] the freedom-loving colonials into a feeling of abhorrence."[30] Although no particular group in the American colonies deserves the "entire credit for having aroused the sentiments that culminated in the adoption of the Bill of Rights' provisions embracing religious liberty," Justice Black noted that Thomas Jefferson, James Madison, and other Virginians "provided a great stimulus and able leadership for the movement."[31] Citing the cases discussed above (especially *Reynolds*), Justice Black reaffirmed the Court's earlier conclusion that the "provisions of the First Amendment, in the drafting and adoption of which Madison and Jefferson played such leading roles, had the same objective and intended to provide the same protection against governmental intrusion on religious liberty as the Virginia [Bill for Religious Liberty]."[32] Thus, the Court's broad interpretations of the First Amendment in cases involving the free exercise clause should apply equally to establishment clause cases. To implement this broad interpretation, Justice Black proposed the following nonexclusive test:

> Neither a state nor the Federal Government can set up a church. Neither can pass laws which aid one religion, aid all religions, or prefer one religion over another. Neither can force nor influence a person to go to or to remain away from church against his will or force him to profess a belief or disbelief in any religion. No person can be punished for entertaining or professing religious beliefs or disbeliefs, for church attendance or non-attendance. No tax in any amount . . . can be levied to support any religious activity or institution, whatever they may be called, or whatever form they may adopt to teach or practice religion. Neither a state nor the Federal Government can, openly or secretly, participate in the affairs of any religious groups and vice versa.[33]

Again citing the *Reynolds* decision, Justice Black summarized by saying, "[I]n the words of Jefferson, the clause against establishment of religion by law was intended to erect 'a wall of separation between Church and State.' "[34]

In applying this establishment clause test, and asserting that the "wall of separation" must be kept "high and impregnable," a majority of the justices decided that the bus fare reimbursement statute did *not* violate the establishment clause. Rather, it merely provided "a general program to help parents get their children, regardless of their religion, safely and expeditiously to and from accredited schools."[35] The purpose of the establishment clause was not to handicap religion, but to require the state "to be a neutral in its relations with groups of religious believers and non-believers."[36]

The Court's decision prompted a vigorous dissent by four of the nine justices. Justice Jackson called the case's "most fitting precedent . . . that of Julia who, according to Byron's reports, 'whispering I will ne'er consent,'—consented."[37] Justice Rutledge's dissenting opinion, joined by Justices Frankfurter, Jackson, and Burton, agreed completely with Justice Black that "the [First] Amendment was the direct culmination" of colonial Virginia's struggle for religious freedom and disestablishment.[38] While earlier opinions of the Supreme Court focused heavily on Thomas Jefferson's efforts, Justice Rutledge gave considerable attention to James Madison's actions as co-author with George Mason of the religion clause in Virginia's Declaration of Rights, primary sponsor of Jefferson's Bill for Religious Freedom, and leader of the opposition to Patrick Henry's bill to provide assessments for teachers of the Christian religion. It was in this last conflict that Madison wrote his "Memorial and Remonstrance" which was, according to Justice Rutledge, "at once the most concise and accurate statement of the views of the First Amendment's author concerning what is 'an establishment of religion.' "[39] Justice Rutledge then described Madison's efforts to have the First Congress adopt a bill of rights.[40] Through Madison's person, Virginia's preconstitutional disestablishmentarianism became embodied in the First Amendment:

> All the great instruments of the Virginian struggle for religious liberty thus became warp and woof of our constitutional tradition, not simply by the course of history, but by the common unifying force of Madison's life, thought and sponsorship. He epitomized the whole of that tradition in the Amendment's compact, but nonetheless comprehensive phrasing.[41]

Thus, the nine justices unanimously interpreted the establishment clause broadly in the context of the Jeffersonian and Madisonian approach; the only question in *Everson* was whether the school bus fare reimbursement program breached the high and impregnable wall of separation. Barely a majority said that it did not.

Two years after *Everson*, another establishment clause case involving schools worked its way to the Supreme Court. In that case, the Court considered a program in Illinois providing for religious teachers (Protestant, Catholic, and Jewish) to come to the public schools once a week during school hours to provide religious teaching to the pupils. For less than an hour, the pupils, with the consent of their parents, were released from secular classes and were permitted to attend the religious instruction. Pupils not attending the religious classes were required to leave their classrooms (where the religious education took place) and take part in secular educational activities elsewhere in the school. This released-time religious education program was approved by the local board of education, and the teachers were subject to the approval of the superintendent of schools.

Without much discussion, the Court, in *Illinois ex rel. McCollum v. Board of Education* (1948),[42] held that the released-time religious education program violated the establishment clause. Justice Black's majority opinion, referring to the *Everson* test, noted that this case clearly involved the "utilization of the tax-established and tax-supported public school system to aid religious groups to spread their faith."[43] The Court rejected the claim that the First Amendment only forbids preference of one religion over another but not the impartial governmental assistance of all religions. Justice Black also noted that the Court's interpretation was not hostile to religion, but that "the First Amendment rests upon the premise that both religion and government can best work to achieve their lofty aims if each is left free from the other within its respective sphere."[44]

Justices Frankfurter, Jackson, Rutledge, and Burton, who dissented from the Court's decision in *Everson*, submitted a concurring opinion in *McCollum*. Taking the majority opinion to task for simply applying the constitutional principle enunciated in *Everson* to the immediate facts of the case, Justice Frankfurter traced the history of American education back to the Massachusetts Bay Colony. According to Justice Frankfurter, the original motivation of the Puritans for education in America was to give children the ability to read the Scriptures. The "modern public school," however, developed from "a philosophy of freedom reflected in the First Amendment." Horace Mann and others (after difficult battles) barred all sectarian influence in public schools, according to Justice Frankfurter, who overlooked the fact that even Horace Mann supported Bible reading in the schools to support moral growth (as we will see in chapter 2). In any event, the justice concluded, "The upshot of these controversies, often long and fierce, is . . . that long before the Fourteenth Amendment subjected the States to new limitations, the prohibition of furtherance by the State of religious instruction became the guiding principle, in law and feeling, of the American people."[45] Thus, according to Justice Frankfurter, the public school became a "symbol of our secular unity. . . . "Designed to serve as perhaps the most powerful agency for promoting cohesion among a heterogeneous democratic people, the public school must keep scrupulously free from entanglement in the strife of sects."[46]

The released-time program grew out of the desire of a variety of religious groups to extend Sunday school during the week, lest religion be viewed as a one-day-a-week obligation. According to Justice Frankfurter, two million pupils in 2,200 communities were participating in some form of released-time program (some were in schools, some were on church property). With this background, the four concurring justices concluded that the Illinois program "presents powerful elements of inherent pressure by the school system in the interest of religious sects."[47]

In his dissenting opinion in *McCollum*, Justice Reed was the first member of the Court to break ranks on its interpretation of the establishment clause. Up to this point, all of the justices had appeared to support the reading of the disestablishmentarian efforts of Jefferson and Madison in Virginia directly into the First Amendment. Referring to Madison's statement in the First Congress that the establishment clause meant that "Congress should not establish a religion, and enforce the legal observation of it by law, nor compel men to worship God in any manner contrary to their conscience," Justice Reed suggested that the "phrase 'an establishment of religion' may have been intended by Congress to be aimed only at a state church."[48] Even if that original intent had been interpreted more broadly in earlier cases, Justice Reed asserted that it had never been interpreted to encompass an optional, extracurricular released-time educational program. He then set out to show that a "reading of the general statements of eminent statesmen of former days . . . will show that circumstances such as those in this case were far from the minds of the authors."[49] For example, according to Thomas Jefferson's regulations for the University of Virginia, students at the university should be free "and expected to attend" religious worship services; thus, according to Justice Reed, Jefferson's "wall of separation" did not exclude religious education from the public university he founded. In Justice Reed's opinion, "A rule of law should not be drawn from a figure of speech."[50] Moreover, Reed said that Madison's "Memorial and Remonstrance" is inapplicable to this case. That great document was written to defeat a tax bill designed to support certain religions. Nothing in the "Memorial and Remonstrance" suggested to Justice Reed any particular conclusions about the constitutionality of religious education in the public schools. This historical background, then, must be weighed against the long-standing practice of released-time religious education in many states. In Justice Reed's view, the Court should give the states "great leeway" in their attempts to deal with "important social problems," and the Court's "[d]evotion to the great principle of religious liberty should not lead us into a rigid interpretation of the constitutional guarantee that conflicts with accepted habits of our people."[51]

Also noteworthy in the *McCollum* case is Justice Jackson's concurring opinion, in which he spoke eloquently of the importance of religion in a variety of elements in American culture. He then punctured the Court's inflated view that constitutional principle and history can simply solve cases such as the one at bar.

> It is idle to pretend that this task is one for which we can find in the Constitution one word to help us as judges to decide where the secular ends and where the sectarian begins in education. Nor can we find guidance in any other legal source. . . . [W]e are likely to make the legal "wall of separation between church and state" as winding as the famous serpentine wall designed by Mr. Jefferson for the University he founded.[52]

Justice Jackson's remarks may seem increasingly apt as we wind our way through subsequent establishment clause cases.

In *Zorach v. Clauson*, the Supreme Court was asked to rule on another released-time religious education program.[53] In that case, decided in 1951, the Court considered a New York City program allowing students to leave school premises once a week, upon their parents' request, to attend religious instruction centers. The religious education was not regulated by the schools in any way, although the religious teachers sent attendance reports to the schools. Opponents of the program argued that it was indistinguishable in principle from the Illinois programs struck down in *McCollum*.

The Supreme Court, however, found dissimilarities between the programs, and held that the program passed constitutional muster. According to the Court's majority opinion by Justice Douglas (speaking for six justices), the New York City schools did "no more than accommodate their schedules to a program of outside religious instruction."[54] Rather than discussing constitutional history, theory, or precedent at length, Justice Douglas focused on the "common sense of the matter." In a passage in which Justice Douglas's examples seem to speak more clearly than his words, the opinion reads:

> The First Amendment . . . does not say that in every and all respects there shall be a separation of Church and State. Rather, it studiously defines the matter, the specific ways, in which there shall be no concert or union or dependency one on the other. . . . Otherwise the state and religion would be aliens to each other—hostile, suspicious, and even unfriendly. Churches could not be required to pay even property taxes. . . . Prayers in our legislative halls; appeals to the Almighty in the messages of the Chief Executive . . . these and all other references to the Almighty that run through our laws, our public rituals, our ceremonies would be flouting the First Amendment.[55]

Justice Douglas then made the pronouncement that is probably second only to the "wall of separation" dictum in its appearance in establishment clause cases: "We are a religious people whose institutions presuppose a Supreme Being." In fact, Justice Douglas proclaimed, "When the state encourages religious instruction or cooperates with religious authorities by adjusting the schedule of public events to sectarian needs, it follows the best of our traditions."[56]

Almost a decade passed before the Supreme Court heard another establishment clause case. In *McGowan v. Maryland* (1961) and its three accompanying cases, the Court considered the constitutionality of Sunday closing laws.[57] The defendants in *McGowan* had been convicted of selling a three-ring loose-leaf binder, a can of floor wax, a stapler and staples, and a toy submarine on a Sunday. Chief Justice Warren's majority opinion recognized that the Sunday laws were originally "motivated by religious forces," but the Court must nevertheless determine whether the current legislation, "having undergone extensive changes from the earliest forms [in the thirteenth century], still retains its religious character."[58] As early as the eighteenth century, commentators such as Sir William Blackstone suggested entirely secular reasons for setting aside a day of rest. In addition, recent Sunday legislation had enjoyed the support of a variety of labor and trade organizations.[59]

Before dealing with the specifics of the Maryland legislation under attack, Chief Justice Warren generally discussed the scope of the establishment clause. Following the Court's approach in *Everson*, he declared that the history of the Virginia bill for establishing religious freedom had been viewed by the Court "as best reflecting the long and intensive struggle for religious freedom in America, [and] as particularly relevant in the search for the First Amendment's meaning."[60] He then noted that in the year James Madison sponsored Jefferson's bill for establishing religious freedom, Madison also presented to the Virginia legislature "A Bill For Punishing . . . Sabbath Breakers" that was also drafted by Thomas Jefferson. Then, after observing that Virginia's Sunday laws had survived a variety of general attacks in Virginia on laws supporting religion, Chief Justice Warren turned to the establishment clause itself. Despite early comments by Justice Joseph Story that the "real object of the amendment was . . . to prevent any national ecclesiastical establishment, which should give to an hierarchy the exclusive patronage of the national government," Chief Justice Warren indicated that the final form of the establishment clause, which forbade laws "*respecting an establishment* of religion," granted the Court license to give the First Amendment a "broad interpretation . . . in the light of its history and the evils it was designed forever to suppress [citing *Everson*]."[61] Nevertheless, Warren noted that "the Establishment Clause does not ban federal or state regulation of conduct whose reason or effect merely happens to coincide or harmonize with the tenets of some or all religions."[62] Despite the religious origins of the Sunday laws, and the fact that they still "harmonize" with Christian beliefs, the Court held the Sunday laws to be in accord with the principles of the First Amendment. "To say that the States cannot prescribe Sunday as a day of rest for these [secular] purposes solely because centuries ago such laws had their genesis in religion would give a constitutional interpretation of hostility to the public welfare rather than one of mere separation of church and state."[63]

The four Sunday law cases generated a great deal of comment by the justices in majority and concurring and dissenting opinions, especially concerning whether the laws violated the free exercise clause. Ultimately, however, at least a majority of the justices concluded in each case that the Sunday laws were not (or, at least, no longer were) religious exercises and, therefore, did not contravene the proscriptions of the establishment clause.

Torcaso v. Watkins (1961), involving the constitutionality of requiring notaries to swear to a belief in God, was tangentially an establishment clause case.[64] Relying on *Zorach v. Clauson* as having silently repudiated the Court's view of the religion clauses in *Everson*, the Maryland courts had sustained the notaries' oath requirement. The Supreme Court disagreed, quoting Justice Frankfurter's concurring opinion in *McCollum* to the effect that "we are all agreed that the First and Fourteenth Amendments have a secular reach far more penetrating in the conduct of Government than merely to forbid an 'established church.' . . . We renew our conviction that 'we have staked the very existence of our country on the faith that complete separation between the state and religion is best for the state and best for religion.' "[65]

The next establishment clause case brought the Supreme Court back to the public schools. The New York Board of Regents had composed a "nondenominational" prayer for use in the schools: "Almighty God, we acknowledge our dependence upon Thee, and we beg Thy blessings upon us, our parents, our teachers, and our Country." A local school board had mandated that each class recite the regents' prayer daily, although students could be excused at their parents' request. In *Engel v. Vitale* (1962), the Court's opinion, written by Justice Black on behalf of five of the justices, declared that the daily classroom prayer was a "religious activity" and that using the public school system to support such a religious activity was unconstitutional.[66] The "nondenominational" and voluntary nature of the prayer would not cure the unconstitutionality because "[t]he Establishment Clause, unlike the Free Exercise Clause, does not depend upon any showing of direct governmental compulsion."[67] Once again, the Court was careful to review the history of church and state in America to guide its interpretation of the establishment clause. "It is a matter of history," argued the Court, "that this very practice of establishing governmentally composed prayers for religious services was one of the reasons which caused many of our early colonists to leave England and seek religious freedom in America."[68] Unfortunately, the freedom-loving colonials Justice Black had extolled in *Everson* turned around in America and established their own state churches and prayers. Many years later, after throwing off the shackles of British political rule, Americans developed an "intense opposition to the practice of establishing religion by law." As a result, the establishment clause was added to the Constitution "to stand as a guarantee that neither the power nor the prestige of the Federal Government would be used to control, support or influence the kinds of prayer the American people can say."[69] Finally, arguing that this decision would not be hostile to religion, the Court was careful to point out in a footnote that the Constitution would not forbid school children from reciting historical documents and patriotic anthems that contain references to God. Nor should the opinion be read as applying to the "many manifestations in our public life of belief in God." Rather, according to Justice Black, "Such patriotic or ceremonial occasions bear no true resemblance to the unquestioned religious exercise [in this case]."[70]

Justice Stewart dissented in *Engel v. Vitale*, arguing that the practice condemned by the majority of the Court was part of the same American tradition as congressional invocations, "God save . . . this Honorable Court" and numerous other examples showing that "we are a religious people whose institutions presuppose a Supreme Being," as Justice Douglas had observed a decade before. In Justice Stewart's opinion, the regents' prayer merely recognized "the deeply intrenched and highly cherished spiritual traditions of our Nation."[71]

Thanks to well-known atheist Madeline Murray O'Hair and several other plaintiffs, the Supreme Court soon again had the chance to deal with religion in the schools and to develop clearer criteria for establishment clause cases. In *School District of Abington Township v. Schempp* (1963), the Court considered whether a state may require Bible readings or the recitation of the Lord's Prayer in the public schools.[72] In holding these practices unconstitutional, Justice Clark's majority opinion began with another reference to the religious character of the American people and the evidence of religious activities in the public realm. Yet, the links between religion and American public life do not overwhelm the importance of religious freedom. As a result, "The views of Madison and Jefferson, preceded by Roger Williams, came to be incorporated not only in the Federal Constitution but likewise in those of most of our States."[73] Reviewing the earlier establishment clause cases, Justice Clark noted that the aim of the Court was to assure that the government treated religion with a "wholesome 'neutrality.' " To achieve the goal of neutrality, the Court developed this test:

> [W]hat are the purpose and the primary effect of the enactment? If either is the advancement or inhibition of religion then the enactment exceeds the scope of legislative power. . . . That is to say that to withstand the strictures of the Establishment Clause there must be a secular legislative purpose and a primary effect that neither advances nor inhibits religion.[74]

In applying this test, the Court held that the Bible reading and Lord's Prayer recitation were religious exercises; therefore, the practices violated the newly formulated establishment clause test. The fact that students could abstain from the exercises did not mitigate the constitutional problems. "Minor encroachments" may well became major invasions of constitutional liberties.[75]

The Court felt constrained to defend its position against the claim that its establishment clause cases established a "religion of secularism," that is, an affirmative hostility to religion. There remains, posited Justice Clark, a place for the study of religion and the Bible: "Nothing we have said here indicates that . . . the study of the Bible [for historical and literary purposes] or of religion, when presented objectively as part of a secular program of education, may not be effected consistently with the First Amendment."[76]

Four justices spoke through concurring opinions in *Schempp*. Justice Douglas concluded that the state's activities were essentially *financing* religious activities, which, he believed, was "the most effective way to establish an institution."[77] Justice Goldberg (joined by Justice Harlan) was concerned that the principle of neutrality (with which he agreed) should not turn into "a brooding and pervasive devotion to the secular and a passive, or even active hostility to the religious," especially since "a vast portion of our people believe in and worship God and . . . many of our legal, political and personal values derive historically from religious teachings."[78]

As in *Engel*, Justice Stewart dissented, arguing that the establishment clause does not forbid communities from choosing to have portions of the Bible read in school classes if students are free not to participate. Rather, the Bible readings should be seen as "measures making possible the free exercise of religion."[79] Justice Stewart's dissenting opinion is also interesting for his views of constitutional history. He interpreted the intent behind the establishment clause as ensuring both that the new federal government would not set up a national church *and* that Congress was powerless to interfere with state establishments (that is, laws "respecting an establishment" would either be favoring a church or interfering with a religion established by a state government). In fact, the justice found it ironical that, as a result of the *Cantwell* case, "a constitutional provision evidently designed to leave the States free to go their own way should now have become a restriction upon their autonomy."[80]

Justice Brennan joined the majority opinion, but not without adding a seventy-five-page discourse on the history of the First Amendment, the Supreme Court's establishment clause cases, and the practice of religion in America. Although generally agreeing with the Court's reliance on James Madison and Thomas Jefferson in its interpretation of the Constitution, Justice Brennan was concerned that the Court should not try to find the answer to every constitutional question in the words of Madison or Jefferson.

> While it is clear to me that the Framers made the Establishment Clause to prohibit more than the creation of an established federal church such as existed in England, I have no doubt that, in their preoccupation with the imminent question of established churches, they gave no distinct consideration to the particular question whether the clausc also forbade devotional exercises in public institutions.[81]

Moreover, Justice Brennan noted, the structure of education had changed considerably since the late eighteenth century, and the nation had become increasingly diverse and religiously plural. "In the face of such profound changes, practices which may have been objectionable to no one in the time of Jefferson and Madison may today be highly offensive to many persons, the deeply devout and nonbelievers alike."[82] As a result, the Court's interpretation of the establishment clause "must necessarily be responsive to the much more highly charged nature of religious questions in contemporary society."[83] And thus Justice Brennan concluded that public school Bible reading violated the establishment clause, although a number of church-state alliances may not contravene the Constitution's mandates: military and prison chaplains, invocations before legislative sessions, nondevotional use of the Bible, certain tax exemptions, certain provisions in public welfare programs (such as benefits to those who are unemployed because of their religious beliefs), and activities with religious origins that no longer have religious meaning (such as "In God We Trust").[84]

The *Engel* and *Schempp* cases touched off enormous public outcry. Many Protestant and Roman Catholic spokespeople lambasted the *Engel* decision. Cardinal Spellman was "shocked and frightened," the Reverend Billy Graham was distraught, and lawyer/bishop James A. Pike lamented that "the Supreme Court has just deconsecrated the nation." Legislative opinion was equally bitter. Senator Ellender referred to the *Schempp* majority as "eight silly old men," Congressman Rooney saw *Engel* as not only "asinine" but a communist threat, and Congressman Andrews summed up the South's reaction to the modern Supreme Court: "They put the Negroes into the schools and now they have driven God out of them."[85] The governors of all but New York called for a constitutional amendment to overturn the *Engel* decision, and Congress held extensive hearings on school prayer amendments in 1962 (after *Engel*) and 1964 (after *Schempp*). No such amendment has yet made it through the Congress, although as recently as 1984, President Reagan lobbied for the following: "Nothing in this Constitution shall be construed to prohibit individual or group prayer in public schools or other public institutions. No person shall be required by the United States or by any State to participate in prayer."[86] Despite the failure of these amendments, prayers have continued to appear in public schools in several parts of the country.[87] As with many issues, from racial integration to interstate commerce, constitutional adjudication is one thing, enforcement is quite another.

Five years passed between *Schempp* and the next establishment clause case, and once again the issue was religion in the public schools. In the 1968 case of *Epperson v. Arkansas*, "Inherit the Wind" made it to the Supreme Court.[88] That great late-night television movie portrayed the courtroom clash of charismatic advocates Clarence Darrow and William Jennings Bryan in *Scopes v. State* (1927), the case in which a teacher was prosecuted for violating the Tennessee law against teaching Darwin's theory of evolution.[89] The *Scopes* case was a national *cause célèbre*, capping years of acrimonious public debate. William Jennings Bryan, for example, regularly debated university professors in the press and offered $100 to any of them who would sign an affidavit that he was personally descended from an ape. Despite Darwinism's rise to scientific prominence by the 1960s, the debate had not been fully extinguished (nor has it yet), and in *Epperson* the constitutional issue was the same as in *Scopes*: May a state forbid teachers in the public schools from teaching evolution?[90] Using the two-part "purpose" and "primary effect" test described in *Schempp*, Justice Fortas's majority opinion concluded that the Arkansas law's purpose was "to blot out a particular theory because of its supposed conflict with the Biblical account, literally read," thus violating the establishment clause.[91]

The next year brought the Court the first in a series of cases that were to become perhaps the most perplexing (if not inconsistent) in the history of constitutional law. The issue was aid to parochial schools, and legislators became increasingly industrious in trying to find ways to help parochial schools, while the opposition (most notably, an organization known as Protestants and Other Americans United for Separation of Church and State) mustered distinguished counsel and multistate efforts to quash these "religious subsidies."

In *Board of Education v. Allen* (1968) the Court considered a state statute requiring the public schools to lend textbooks, at no charge, to students attending grades seven through twelve at private schools.[92] Using the "purpose" and "primary effect" tests outlined in *Schempp*, the Court upheld the textbook loan program. Rather than seeing the program as a sponsorship of nonpublic (and usually parochial) education, a majority of the justices focused on the benefits to the school children and their families. This "child benefit" theory can be summarized as follows:

> (1) the statute merely made available to all children the benefits of a general program to lend school books free of charge, (2) books were furnished at the request of the pupil and ownership remained at least technically in the state, (3) no funds or books were furnished to parochial schools, (4) the financial benefit was to the parents and children rather than to the schools, (5) only secular books could receive approval for loans and (6) the statute was not alleged in any way to have coerced the plaintiffs as individuals in the practice of their religion.[93]

Thus for the second time in two occasions (the first being the *Everson* case), the Supreme Court upheld a state program designed to aid private schools. This trend did not last long, however. After *Allen*, the Court's interpretive approach evolved, and later legislation aiding parochial schools fared much worse, at least at the primary and secondary school levels.

The next time the Supreme Court considered the establishment clause, it faced a historical precedent antedating the First Amendment itself. In *Walz v. Tax Commission* (1970), the Court had to decide whether state real property tax exemptions for religious organizations contravened the establishment clause. These kinds of exemptions dated back to the colonial era and continued in effect in all fifty states.

Before venturing into the merits of the case, Chief Justice Burger's majority opinion reflected on the "internal inconsistency" in prior establishment clause cases deriving from what "may have been too sweeping utterances [having] limited meaning as general principles."[94] The Chief Justice then stated the "general principle" deducible from all of the Court's opinions dealing with the religion clauses of the First Amendment:

> [W]e will not tolerate either governmentally established religion or governmental interference with religion. Short of those expressly proscribed governmental acts there is room for play in the joints productive of a benevolent neutrality which will permit religious exercise to exist without sponsorship and without interference.[95]

"Benevolent neutrality" soon became the motto of the legions of Americans who urged the Court to allow Congress and the states to provide support for religion.

Having thus apologized for the Court's treatment of the establishment clause, the Chief Justice turned to the legislative purpose of the tax exemption, which he asserted was "neither the advancement nor the inhibition of religion."[96] Rather, it merely spared religious (and other not-for-profit) institutions from the burden of property taxes. But examining legislative purpose is not the end of the inquiry: "We must also be sure that the end result—the effect—is not an excessive government entanglement with religion."[97] Excessive entanglement is necessarily a matter of degree, and Justice Burger focused the inquiry on "whether [the involvement] is a continuing one calling for official and continuing surveillance leading to an impermissible degree of entanglement."[98] Without providing much further amplification, the Chief Justice turned to Oliver Wendell Holmes's aphorism, "[A] page of history is worth a volume of logic."[99] Choosing the page of history, Justice Burger observed that the tax exemption had a 200 year history in America and had shown no signs of leading to an established church.

Justice Harlan submitted a concurring opinion in *Walz* that introduced another element periodically raised thereafter in establishment clause cases: political divisiveness. According to Justice Harlan, "[G]overnmental involvement [with religion], while neutral, may be so direct or in such degree as to engender a risk of politicizing religion." History, concluded the justice, "cautions that political fragmentation on sectarian lines must be guarded against."[100] Justice Harlan found that the broad tax exemption (which included religious and secular charitable organizations) did not create an unconstitutional sectarian political conflict. Unfortunately, despite the Court's penchant for footnotes (following the obfuscatory pattern of the law reviews) Justice Harlan cited only a *Harvard Law Review* article by Professor Paul Freund who cited nothing at all to support the proposition that the "risk of politicizing religion" can (or should) be a constitutional infirmity.[101]

Justice Douglas dissented vigorously in *Walz*, arguing that tax exemption and state subsidy were two sides of the same coin. For the second time in establishment clause jurisprudence, James Madison's eloquent "Memorial and Remonstrance," written in opposition to a Virginia assessment for teachers of the Christian religion, was appended to a justice's opinion. (The first time was in Justice Rutledge's dissenting opinion in *Everson*.) Justice Douglas saw this financial assistance as a far cry from the *Zorach v. Clauson* type of accommodation he had encouraged almost twenty years earlier.[102]

The next case, a parochial school aid case especially important for its development of First Amendment doctrine, was *Lemon v. Kurtzman* (1971). *Lemon* involved a challenge to a Pennsylvania program of reimbursing private schools for teacher's salaries, books, and materials used in certain secular subjects and a Rhode Island program granting a fifteen percent salary supplement to teachers in private schools.

Once again, Chief Justice Burger assigned himself the task of writing the majority opinion in which he said, "[W]e can only dimly perceive the lines of demarcation in this extraordinarily sensitive area of constitutional law."[103] Focusing on the "respecting an establishment" language in the First Amendment, Justice Burger noted that a law "might not *establish* a state religion but nevertheless be one 'respecting' that end in the sense of being a step that could lead to such establishment and hence offend the First Amendment."[104] In other words, where Justice Stewart in *Engel* suggested that the language "respecting an establishment" was so drafted to *limit* Congress's ability to inhibit state establishments, Justice Burger saw the same language as *expanding* the Court's power to do just that.

With this broad reading in mind, Justice Burger, for the first of many times in establishment clause cases, articulated a three-part test: "First, the statute must have a secular legislative purpose; second, its principal or primary effect must be one that neither advances nor inhibits religion; . . . finally, the statute must not foster 'an excessive government entanglement with religion.' "[105] This tripartite test combined the "purpose" and "primary effect" tests of *Schempp* with the "excessive entanglement" test that surfaced in Chief Justice Burger's majority opinion in *Walz* (although in *Walz* the entanglement test appeared only to be a part of the "primary effect" inquiry).

In applying these tests, the chief justice quickly concluded that the Pennsylvania and Rhode Island statutes had the secular legislative purpose of fostering high-quality secular education in all schools. The states even had complicated statutory precautions designed to ensure that the effect of the statutes would not advance religion. Yet it was those careful precautions that became the statutes' downfall since the Court concluded that they created an excessive entanglement between government and religion.[106]

Although prior cases, such as *Everson* and *Allen*, had permitted the states to provide parochial school students with bus transportation, secular books, and a handful of other things, this case dealt with salary subsidies. Parochial schools, run by the Roman Catholic church with nuns and priests as teachers, created a more complicated situation. As the Court noted, "[A] textbook's content is ascertainable, but a teacher's handling of a subject is not."[107] The states recognized the obligation to ensure that their programs did not run counter to the Constitution by supporting the teaching of religion, and they set up careful restrictions. In Rhode Island, for example, eligible recipients could teach only courses offered in the public schools and use public school texts, and they were forbidden from teaching courses in religion. But these restrictions were flawed by their very existence. "Comprehensive, discriminating, and continuing state surveillance" would be necessary to monitor compliance with these requirements, thus creating an unconstitutional entanglement between church and state.[108]

Not content with invalidating these programs solely on ministerial grounds, Chief Justice Burger reached back to Justice Harlan's opinion in *Walz* and included the potential for political divisiveness within the entanglement test. According to the chief justice, "[P]olitical division along religious lines was one of the principal evils against which the First Amendment was intended to protect. . . . The potential divisiveness of such conflict is a threat to the normal political process."[109] To allow religiously inspired debate in the legislatures would divert attention from the other local and national issues of "great urgency." Unfortunately, the chief justice provided no more elucidation than did his colleague Justice Harlan in developing the political divisiveness analysis.

Justice Douglas (joined by Justice Black) issued a strongly worded concurring opinion condemning the Rhode Island and Pennsylvania programs as a tax in support of religion, a theme sounding throughout many of Justice Douglas's opinions in establishment clause cases.[110] Justice Brennan also contributed a concurring opinion in which he called again for an interpretation of the establishment clause that "accords with history and faithfully reflects the understanding of the Founding Fathers."[111] He summarized that original intent as proscribing "those involvements of religions with secular institutions which (a) serve the essentially religious activities of religious institutions; (b) employ the organs of government for essentially religious purposes; or (c) use essentially religious means to serve governmental ends, where secular means would suffice."[112] In the Rhode Island and Pennsylvania salary supplement programs, Justice Brennan found a direct government subsidy of sectarian organizations. This close relationship between church and state creates dangers for both. One parochial school teacher, for example, stopped praying with his class to make sure that religion stayed out of his subsidized classroom. Because the statutes involved the state in the religious activities of religious institutions (part one of Justice Brennan's test), they were unconstitutional.[113]

Another case involving aid to religious education, *Tilton v. Richardson* (1971), was decided on the same day as *Lemon*.[114] *Tilton* is probably most noteworthy for showing how much trouble these cases have posed for the Court. In a five to four decision in which the chief justice could only get the support of three other justices for his plurality opinion, the Court barely upheld a federal law providing construction grants for college buildings used for secular purposes. The law was challenged on the grounds that it unconstitutionally provided government funding for religious colleges.

The precise reasoning in *Tilton* and the myriad of similar cases following in the same vein has contributed little to clarifying the establishment clause doctrine that Chief Justice Burger thought was sadly confused and inconsistent a year earlier.[115] In each parochial school aid case, the Court employed the three-part test formally announced in *Lemon*, and often the cases turned on seemingly inconsequential differences among the statutory programs. Reimbursement for bus trips to religious schools are permissible but not for field trips.[116] States may lend textbooks to parochial schools, but not tape recorders.[117] By and large, except for the early cases of *Everson* and *Allen*, the Court has been hostile to any type of aid to religious elementary and secondary schools. Without admitting that a line has been drawn at the end of twelfth grade, however, the Court has upheld a variety of programs to aid higher education in colleges and universities sponsored by religious organizations. These school aid cases have drawn the ire of scholars who have described them as everything from a "drunkard's reel" to Hansel and Gretel's forest after the birds ate the crumbs.[118]

Thanks to the parochial school aid issue, June 25, 1973, was an eventful day for the establishment clause. The High Court handed down decisions in nine cases all striking down programs granting state funds to private schools or to parents of private school students. At the same time, however, the Court upheld a South Carolina revenue bond program to provide funds for a Baptist College at Charleston.[119] In each case, the result was determined by an application of the three-part establishment clause test. And once again, it appeared that the Court's wall of separation between high school and college was even more solid than the one between church and state.

Most of the establishment clause analysis came in Justice Powell's majority opinion in *Committee for Public Education v. Nyquist* and its three companion cases, all dealing with a New York education law granting funds for the maintenance and repair of certain private schools and providing tuition reimbursements and tax benefits to parents of private school students. Justice Powell began his opinion with another reference to Madison and Jefferson whose "strongly held convictions" are reflected in the establishment clause.[120] Acknowledging the perplexing nature of the Court's establishment clause jurisprudence, Justice Powell nevertheless noted that "the controlling constitutional standards have become firmly rooted and the broad contours of our work are now well defined."[121] After citing virtually every establishment clause case decided to date, Justice Powell came to the well-established three-part test, calling it "a product of considerations derived from the full sweep of the Establishment Clause cases."[122]

Since Justice Powell's opinion found problems under the "primary effect" and "excessive entanglement" parts of the test, it did not devote much time to the statute's purpose. Rather, he noted that the New York legislature had appended to the bill a list of secular interests revolving around the need for a healthy and safe educational environment for all of the state's children.

The maintenance and repair grants flunked the primary effect test, however, because there was no restriction against using the funds to repair a chapel. Thus, "their effect, inevitably, is to subsidize and advance the religious mission of sectarian schools" in violation of the establishment clause.[123] This analysis required Justice Powell to walk carefully through the maze of earlier cases, especially *Allen* and *Everson*, in which the Court upheld programs benefiting parochial schools every bit as much as limited maintenance and repair grants.

The tuition reimbursement and tax relief programs ran afoul of the "primary effect" test for largely the same reasons. The Court was not persuaded that the constitutional result should change because the benefits inured to the parents rather than to the school.

Perhaps more interesting than the grounds for the Court's decision was the gratuitous commentary Justice Powell added on the political divisiveness aspect of the entanglement test. Observing that it was not necessary to discuss entanglement, the justice said,

> [T]he importance of the competing societal interests . . . prompts us to make the further observation that, apart from any specific entanglement of the State in particular religious programs, assistance of the sort here involved carries grave potential for entanglement in the broader sense of continuing political strife over aid to religion.[124]

The potential for political divisiveness, according to Justice Powell, lay in the likelihood that the parochial school aid programs would become entrenched and escalate in both cost and political strife. He did not, however, elevate political divisiveness to equal status with the three parts of the test, noting that although "the prospect of such divisiveness may not alone warrant the invalidation of state laws that otherwise survive the careful scrutiny required by the decisions of this Court, it is certainly a 'warning signal' not to be ignored."[125] If nothing else then, the political divisiveness "test" is the Court's "warning signal" to legislatures contemplating aid to parochial schools.

Nyquist and its accompanying cases generated a spate of dissenting and concurring opinions in which justices opted for and against the various parochial school aid programs. Justice Burger, for example, harkened once again (as in *Walz*) to "experience and history" rather than logic to support the "fundamental principle" that the establishment clause "does not forbid governments, state or federal, to enact a program of general welfare under which benefits are distributed to private individuals, even though many of those individuals may elect to use those benefits in ways that 'aid' religious instruction or worship."[126] Accordingly, the tuition reimbursement programs and tax credits should stand in the tradition of cases such as *Everson*, *Allen* and *Quick Bear v. Leupp*.

Justice White was also reluctant to strike down the New York parochial school aid programs, at least on their face. But the most noteworthy aspect of his dissenting opinion was his frank acknowledgment that the courts have "fashioned answers to [church-state] questions as best they can, the language of the Constitution and its history having left them a wide range of choice among many alternatives." Ultimately, the courts "carved out what they deemed to be the most desirable national policy."[127] With this kind of bold acknowledgment that the Court has taken on a policy-making role in church-state cases, it is no wonder that one scholar has described the Court's parochial school aid cases as "The Supreme Court as National School Board."[128] As *Nyquist* and other parochial school aid cases multiplied and divided the Court even further, the careful walk through the maze came more and more to resemble the "drunkard's reel."

The flurry of these cases in the 1970s did not completely supplant the issue of religion in the public schools. Almost two decades after *Engel* and *Schempp*, the court decided *Stone v. Graham* (1980), a case involving a Kentucky statute requiring that the Ten Commandments be posted in each public school classroom.[129] In a brief per curiam opinion, the Court struck down the statute because it had no secular legislative purpose even though the commandments had to be accompanied by a statement that "The secular application of the Ten Commandments is clearly seen in its adoption as the fundamental legal code of Western Civilization and the Common Law of the United States."[130] Noting that the Ten Commandments are a "sacred text" for Jews and Christians, and that they include mandates to love God, avoid idolatry, observe the Sabbath, and similar matters, the Court concluded that the law served no educational function, and thus no secular purpose.

In the cases from *McCollum* through *Stone v. Graham*, the Supreme Court had outlawed released-time in-school religion classes, school prayers,

Bible reading, religiously controlled science instruction, and classroom posters advertising the Ten Commandments. But the war over religion in the public schools was not over. Another approach soon became popular: equal access.

"Equal access" means that public schools having activity periods (or after-school programs) that are open to a wide range of voluntary student activities must allow student religious groups to participate on an equal footing with secular organizations. Although equal access has existed in some communities for a number of years, it became the subject of considerable national attention in 1984 when Congress enacted legislation requiring school districts receiving federal funds to adopt an equal access policy.[131]

Although the constitutionality of equal access in the public schools was not determined until almost ten years later, the Supreme Court dealt with the issue at the college level in 1981. In *Widmar v. Vincent* (1981), the Court heard a challenge to a policy of the University of Missouri at Kansas City denying student religious groups the opportunity to use the university's facilities.[132] The bulk of Justice Powell's majority opinion discussed how the university had created an "open public forum" by permitting a wide variety of student groups access to its buildings and grounds. As a result, the Constitution's free speech and association mandates required the university to provide that access on a nondiscriminatory basis unless it could show a compelling state interest.

Unlike most church-state cases in which a state action is attacked on establishment clause grounds, this case involved the University of Missouri using the clause in defense of its policy of discriminating against religious groups. The Court disagreed. The purpose and entanglement tests would be "clearly met" by an equal access policy. And the primary effect of creating a "public forum, open to all forms of discourse, would [not] be to advance religion."[133] Rather, any benefit to religion would be "incidental" since the benefits would be provided to a very broad spectrum of student organizations. Unless the university could produce "empirical evidence" that religious groups would dominate the public forum, then, the open access policy would pass all three elements of the establishment clause test.

The next establishment clause case veered away from the schools into uncharted waters. The State of Minnesota had amended its charitable contributions law to exempt from some registration and reporting requirements only religious organizations that obtain more than fifty percent of their contributions from members. The Holy Spirit Association for the Unification of World Christianity challenged the law on constitutional grounds. The plaintiffs argued that the law contradicted the establishment clause's mandates by favoring one type of religion over another. In a five to four decision, the Court agreed.

This case, *Larson v. Valente* (1982), gave Justice Brennan, author of several noteworthy concurring and dissenting opinions in establishment clause cases, a chance to write the majority opinion.[134] His premise was: "The clearest command of the Establishment Clause is that one religious denomination cannot be officially preferred over another."[135] Because the Minnesota statute created such a preference, it must be struck down, "unless it is justified by a compelling governmental interest . . . and unless it is closely fitted to further that interest."[136] Justice Brennan then concluded that the state's interest in protecting its citizens from unscrupulous solicitations for charity was a valid and compelling purpose, but that the statute's fifty percent rule was not logically or closely fitted to that interest.

Perhaps more interesting than Justice Brennan's analysis of the statute per se is his attempt to squeeze his rationale into the three-part test. Noting that "application of the [three-part test] is not necessary to the disposition" of this case, the entanglement prong is "the most directly implicated," especially as it reflects concern over political divisiveness.[137] The Minnesota statute, by its "very nature" created the risk of politicizing religion."[138] Its "religious gerrymandering" was simply too apparent to Justice Brennan as he quoted from the legislative floor debate in which one senator said, "I'm not sure why we're so hot to regulate the Moonies anyway."[139] Justice White, in dissent, pounced on Justice Brennan's facile attempt to invoke the three-part test, asserting that the majority opinion had essentially limited the three-part test to the consideration of laws benefitting all religions as opposed to those with discriminatory provisions.[140] Neither he nor Justice Brennan, however, broached the issue of whether saying prayers, reading the Bible, or posting the Ten Commandments applied to all religions. The unstated assumption—here and in many establishment clause cases—was that ostensibly nondenominational religious activities do not discriminate among religions.

Following on *Larson*'s heels was another establishment clause case most noteworthy because the High Court bothered to hear it. A Massachusetts law gave churches and schools the power to veto any application for a liquor license within 500 feet of their establishments. The imaginative plaintiff attacked this statute on the grounds that it not only violated the establishment clause and the equal protection and due process clauses of the Constitution but also the Sherman Antitrust Act. In *Larkin v. Grendel's Den* (1982), Chief Justice Burger's majority opinion declared the law to be a violation of the establishment clause.[141]

Citing historical sources as diverse as Bernard Bailyn's *Ideological Origins of the American Revolution* and Webb's *The History of Liquor Licensing in England*, Justice Burger found problems under the effect and entanglement prongs of the three-part establishment clause test. Not only were there no standards by which a church must exercise its veto, but "the mere appearance of a joint exercise of legislative authority by Church and

State provides a significant symbolic benefit to religion in the minds of some by reason of the power conferred."[142] Finally, the law "enmeshes churches in the processes of government" and threatens political divisiveness, thus creating an unconstitutional entanglement of church and state.[143]

A few months after *Grendel's Den*, the Court appeared to be squarely on the horns of a dilemma. The practice at issue, legislative chaplains, was probably more clearly unconstitutional under existing precedents than any state action yet seen by the Court, but at the same time had even more pages of history in its favor than the tax exemptions upheld in *Walz*. After all, the First Congress had appointed a paid chaplain three days *before* approving the Bill of Rights, and chaplains have served federal and state legislatures ever since.

The Court quickly removed itself from the uncomfortable horns. In a remarkably short opinion essentially void of establishment clause analysis, Justice Burger announced the Court's decision, in *Marsh v. Chambers* (1983), to uphold Nebraska's practice of paying a legislative chaplain.[144] Noting that prayers in the legislature have become "part of the fabric of our society," Justice Burger concluded that it would be incongruous to impose stricter standards on the states than the First Congress imposed on itself.[145] As a result, the legislative chaplaincy practice is "a tolerable acknowledgment of beliefs widely held among the people of this country" even though the Nebraska chaplains for the last sixteen years have all been Presbyterian clergymen and the prayers were "in the Judeo-Christian tradition."[146]

Not surprisingly, this decision spawned dissenting opinions. Justice Brennan, for example, observed that any group of law students would quickly find the chaplaincy practice unconstitutional under the three-part test. Having lost this battle, Justice Brennan was forced to maintain a rearguard action to keep the wall of separation from crumbling under the weight of Justice Burger's tomes of history. He announced that the chief justice had written "a narrow and, on the whole, careful opinion," in which legislative chaplains were essentially exempted from the establishment clause's mandates. Thus, he posited, "[T]he Court is carving out an exception to the Establishment Clause rather than reshaping Establishment Clause doctrine."[147]

Justice Brennan then took the opportunity to comment generally on the "underlying function" of the establishment clause and "the forces that have shaped its doctrine." Fundamentally, he argued, the establishment clause is different from most of the provisions of the Bill of Rights because it does not "arise out of moral intuitions applicable to individuals as well as governments." Rather, it is a "statement about the proper role of *government* in the society."[148] The dual principles of "separation" and "neutrality" embodied in the establishment clause serve to guarantee freedom of conscience, to keep the government from interfering with religious life or institutions, to prevent the "trivialization and degradation" of religion by too close contact with the state, and to ensure that religious issues not create battles in the political arena.[149] There are, however, tensions within the first amendment that make the hard-and-fast approach of separation and neutrality inappropriate in some cases. For example, some programs incidentally aiding religion as part of general benefits legislation have been upheld, as have governmental acts coinciding with religious beliefs (such as the Sunday laws upheld in *McGowan*). Moreover, tax exemptions for churches have been upheld to avoid the risks inherent in the government becoming entangled administratively with religion by subjecting churches to taxation. Finally, "[T]he Constitution is *not* neutral on the subject of religion: Under the Free Exercise Clause, religiously motivated claims of conscience may give rise to constitutional rights that other strongly-held beliefs do not."[150] Justice Brennan stopped short of creating a formal philosophical basis for the establishment clause and its treatment by the Court, merely noting that the practice of paying legislative chaplains did not fall within any of the areas in which the principles of separation and neutrality had been tempered by other concerns.

In addressing the constitutional exception granted to legislative chaplains, Justice Brennan argued not only that history was "profoundly unilluminating" but more importantly that "the argument tendered by the Court is misguided because the Constitution is not a static document whose meaning on every detail is fixed for all time by the life experience of the Framers."[151] Quoting his concurring opinion in *Schempp*, Justice Brennan argued that "our religious composition makes us a vastly more diverse people than were our forefathers. . . . In the face of such profound changes, practices which may have been objectionable to no one in the time of Jefferson and Madison may today be highly offensive to many persons, the deeply devout and the nonbelievers alike."[152]

Finally, Justice Brennan defended himself from the attack that the separation of church and state "robs the nation of its spiritual identity."[153] Although individuals may not be able to be neutral on the subject of religion (according to philosopher William James), government must be. Citing Alexis de Tocqueville, Justice Brennan argued that the "spirits of religion and of freedom" are inevitably linked in America. Had the Court struck down Nebraska's legislative chaplaincy program, the spirit of religion and the spirit of freedom would have both been "invigorated" by the public response.[154]

Although the High Court's members found plenty of opportunity to generate controversy in *Marsh* and *Grendel*'s Den, the cases themselves related to situations rarely touching most Americans. This was hardly true in the Supreme Court's next opportunity to repoint the wall between church and state. In *Lynch v. Donnelly* (1984), several Pawtucket, Rhode Island, residents had filed suit to challenge the city's annual Christmas display that featured a nativity scene depicting the birth of Jesus along with Santa Claus and a variety of other seasonal figures.[155] The crèche, which was of nominal value, had been erected on private property for the past forty years. The plaintiffs did not attack the entire display; instead they focused on the religious nature of the manger scene as a violation of the establishment clause.

Chief Justice Burger, once again writing the majority opinion, spurned this opportunity to take Christ out of Christmas. Resurrecting the Court's 1952 *Zorach* opinion, the chief justice emphasized that the Constitution "affirmatively mandates accommodation, not merely tolerance, of all religions, and forbids hositility toward any."[156] Then the Court followed the *Marsh* style of historical analysis and noted both the First Congress's appointment of a chaplain and the "unbroken history of official acknowledgment by all three branches of government of the role of religion in American life."[157] Rejecting an "absolutist" approach to the First Amendment, Chief Justice Burger invoked the well-known three-part test with much less reverence than usual. Although the Supreme Court had "often found it useful" to inquire into secular purpose, primary effect, and entanglement, "we have repeatedly emphasized our unwillingness to be confined to any single test or criterion in this sensitive area."[158] Then, in examining these "useful" criteria, Justice Burger concluded that the depiction of the origins of Christmas was a valid secular purpose and that the primary effect was of less benefit to religion than the legislative prayers upheld in *Marsh* and the entanglement between church and state was minimal. Moreover, the chief justice rejected the trial court's reliance on political divisiveness, pointing out that the Supreme Court had never invalidated a practice solely on that basis.[159] In fact, since the case did not involve "a direct subsidy to church-sponsored schools or colleges, or other religious institutions . . . no inquiry into political divisiveness is even called for."[160] Finally, obviously responding to criticism in dissenting opinions and in commentary, Justice Burger reiterated his belief that cases such as *McCollum*, *Epperson*, *Stone v. Graham*, and others had "abundantly demonstrate[d] the Court's concern to protect the genuine objectives of the Establishment Clause."[161] But, the crèche, taken in its holiday context, must withstand constitutional challenge.

Justice O'Connor concurred in the majority's decision but submitted an opinion to "suggest a clarification of [the Court's] Establishment Clause doctrine."[162] Justice O'Connor's approach is simply stated:

> The Establishment Clause prohibits government from making adherence to a religion relevant in any way to a person's standing in the political community. Government can run afoul of that prohibition in two principal ways. One is excessive entanglement with religious institutions, which may interfere with the independence of the institutions, give [them] access to government or governmental powers not

fully shared by non adherents of the religion, and foster the creation of political constituencies defined along religious lines. . . . The second and more direct infringement is government endorsement or disapproval of religion.[163]

The traditional three-part test must then be interpreted (that is, replaced, were the Court not so reluctant to abandon even unwieldy frameworks) by this two-part entanglement/endorsement inquiry. The purpose and effect elements of the test are thus bases for determining the extent of governmental endorsement of religion, which, according to Justice O'Connor, was not present in a "celebration of the public holiday through its traditional symbols."[164]

Once again, Justice Brennan issued a lengthy and thoughtful dissenting opinion (joined by Justices Marshall, Blackmun, and Stevens). As in *Marsh*, he emphasized the narrowness of the Court's ruling in light of the particular circumstances of the case. Diligently working to shore up the faltering tripartite test, Justice Brennan concluded that "this case appears hard not because the principles of decision are obscure, but because the Christmas holiday seems so familiar and agreeable."[165]

One of the most remarkable cases in establishment clause history is *Wallace v. Jaffree* (1985), with the action beginning at the trial court level. Judge Brevard Hand of the Southern District of Alabama was asked to stop public school teachers from leading classroom prayers and to enjoin an Alabama law setting forth a homeroom prayer and permitting teachers to "announce that a period of silence not to exceed one minute in duration shall be observed for meditation or voluntary prayer."[166] Governor Fob James defended the law on the grounds that prayer flows from the Almighty and no court has jurisdiction over the requirements of the Lord. Judge Hand issued a temporary injunction based on his oath of office to uphold the laws of the United States and the principles of stare decisis which required him to follow Supreme Court precedents such as *Engel* and *Schempp*.[167] But after hearing the evidence and familiarizing himself with recent works of historical scholarship, the judge changed his views and boldly declared that "the establishment clause of the First Amendment to the United States Constitution does not bar the states from establishing a religion."[168] He based this conclusion on two historical arguments. First, noting the existence of congressional chaplains and other convergences of religion and government in the late eighteenth century, the judge held that the Founding Fathers "never intended the establishment clause to erect an absolute wall of separation between the federal government and religion."[169] And second, the judge said that the nineteenth-century Congress did not intend for the Fourteenth Amendment to incorporate the provisions of the establishment clause; therefore, since the establishment clause refers only to the United States Congress, the states are free to establish one or more religions.

Not surprisingly, in an appeal on the homeroom prayer portion of the law, the Supreme Court unanimously rejected the trial judge's "remarkable conclusion that the Federal Constitution imposes no obstacle to Alabama's establishment of a state religion."[170] The Court had a little more difficulty, however, when it came to the minute of silence provisions. Ultimately, the Court struck down the Alabama law, but five of the nine justices suggested that they would permit a minute of silence law under the proper conditions.

Despite the wide spectrum of opinions on the minute of silence, none of the justices supported Judge Hand's assertion that the establishment clause fails to address state actions. Justice Stevens's majority opinion, in fact, began by acknowledging "how firmly embedded in our constitutional jurisprudence is the proposition that the several states have no greater power to restrain the individual freedoms protected by the First Amendment than does the Congress."[171] Justice Stevens also supported the Court's precedents in establishment clause cases, particularly with respect to the three-part test. In this case, he concluded, the first prong—secular purpose—was not satisfied since the Alabama statute's legislative history was replete with statements evidencing a distinctly religious intent.

Justice Powell issued a concurring opinion in which he both defended the use of the three-part test and said that he would vote to uphold a minute of silence law with a valid secular purpose. Justice O'Connor then reiterated her suggestion in *Lynch* that the Court adopt an endorsement/entanglement inquiry, with endorsement being at issue in *Wallace v. Jaffree*. She said, the "crucial question is whether the State has conveyed or attempted to convey the message that children should use the moment of silence for prayer."[172] The state legislatures should be given considerable deference and just "a plausible secular purpose" in either the text or legislative history should be sufficient. In this case, however, Alabama "intentionally crossed the line between creating a quiet moment during which those so inclined may pray, and affirmatively endorsing the particular religious practice of prayer."[173]

The Court's decision in *Wallace v. Jaffree* inspired several justices to dissent. Chief Justice Burger's dissenting opinion, for example, demonstrates primarily his impatience with the Court for being hostile to religion, misinterpreting the legislative history, and being excessively devoted to the three-part test.[174] But the most important aspect of *Wallace v. Jaffree* was the call by Justice Rehnquist (who was soon to be appointed as chief justice), joined in principle by Justice White, for a complete revamping of the Court's treatment of the establishment clause. Harking back to the *Reynolds* and *Everson* decisions in which the Court invoked Thomas Jefferson's "wall of separation" metaphor to describe the First Amendment's religion clauses, Rehnquist asserted, "It is impossible to build sound constitutional doctrine upon a mistaken understanding of constitutional history."[175]

In a lengthy discussion of the legislative history of the establishment clause, Justice Rehnquist concluded that "the evil to be aimed at . . . appears to have been the establishment of a national church, and perhaps the preference of one religious sect over another; but it was definitely not concern about whether the Government might aid all religions evenhandedly."[176] Postenactment executive actions, such as national days of prayer and fasting, thanksgiving days, and aid to sectarian schools for Indian education, lend further support for this interpretation, according to Justice Rehnquist.[177] Ultimately, he concluded, that there is "simply no historical foundation for the proposition that the Framers intended to build the 'wall of separation' that was constitutionalized in *Everson*."[178] Instead, Rehnquist suggested, the Court must abandon the three-part test and return to a true reading of the Founding Fathers' original intent, leading it to conclude that nondiscriminatory aid to religion is fully compatible with the establishment clause.

The next case, *Estate of Thornton v. Caldor* (1985), took the Court away from the politically charged realm of school prayer to a Connecticut statute reading, "No person who states that a particular day of the week is observed as his Sabbath may be required to work on such day."[179] In a brief opinion in which Chief Justice Burger invoked the three-part test for "guidance," the Court (by an eight to one majority with Justice Rehnquist in dissent) held the statute unconstitutional because it had a "primary effect that impermissibly advances a particular religious practice."[180] Chief Justice Burger was particularly concerned that there were no exceptions to the law in cases where compliance would cause undue hardship on employers. Similarly, Justice O'Connor, in her concurring opinion, singled out the absolute nature of the law as an "endorsement of a particular religious belief," thus running afoul of her proposed "endorsement" test.[181]

By July of 1985, the Court was back to the educational arena where so many church-state battles have been fought. In *Grand Rapids School District v. Ball*, several Michigan taxpayers challenged both "shared time" and "community education" programs offered in Grand Rapids.[182] In the shared time program, nonpublic school students were given remedial or enrichment courses by full-time public school teachers in classrooms at the private schools that were leased to the public schools. The community education program was offered to students and adults in nonpublic schools at the end of the school day in classrooms leased to the public schools. The teachers were frequently recruited from the ranks of the private schools where they continued to teach when not teaching the after-school community education classes.

Justice Brennan's majority opinion noted that although the three-part test was only a "guideline," the Court has "particularly relied on [it] in every case involving the sensitive relationship between government and religion in the education of our children."[183] Measuring the Michigan programs against these standards, Justice Brennan first upheld their "manifestly secular" purpose. In evaluating the programs' effect and likelihood of government entanglement with religion, however, he focused on the fact that forty of the forty-one eligible nonpublic schools were "identifiably religious" and "pervasively sectarian." As a result, there were three significant problems: the teachers might become involved in religious indoctrination, the programs might create "a crucial symbolic link between government and religion," and the programs might provide a subsidy to the "primary religious mission" of the schools.[184] Citing many of the parochial school aid cases, Justice Brennan concluded that these attributes of the programs created a violation of the establishment clause.[185]

On the same day in 1985, the Court issued its decision in a very similar case, *Aguilar v. Felton*, in which taxpayers challenged a New York approach resembling Grand Rapids's shared time program.[186] Once again, in a majority opinion by Justice Brennan, the program was struck down despite a system designed by the state to monitor the religious content of the publicly funded classes. In fact, Justice Brennan pointed to the monitoring system as not only creating an excessive entanglement, but also producing a risk of "political divisiveness along religious lines."[187]

The Chief Justice dissented on the grounds that invalidating the essentially harmless programs "has no support in logic, experience or history," and manifested a hostility towards religion.[188] Justice Rehnquist issued yet another dissenting opinion slamming the Supreme Court's establishment clause jurisprudence, and Justice O'Connor argued that the New York program should pass muster even under the three-part test.[189]

In a rare moment of establishment clause unanimity, the nine justices voted to uphold a Washington vocational rehabilitation program that had been struck down by that state's highest court. In *Witters v. Washington Department of Services for the Blind* (1986), the Court upheld the constitutionality of state funding for the petitioner to attend the Inland Empire School of the Bible to become a pastor, missionary, or youth director.[190] The state program was established to " '[p]rovide special education and/or training in the professions, business or trades' so as to assist visually handicapped persons to overcome vocational handicaps and to obtain the maximum degree of self-support and self-care."[191] Larry Witters, petitioner, was eligible for the program, but the state agency refused to provide aid for those pursuing careers in religion. The Washington Supreme Court concurred, finding that "the provision of financial assistance by the State to enable someone to become a pastor, missionary, or church youth director clearly has the primary effect of advancing religion" and therefore violates the *Lemon* test.[192] Justice Marshall wrote the Court's opinion reversing the Washington court's decision. Noting that the Court is "guided" by the *Lemon* test, he addressed the "principal or primary effect" test by pointing out that "the decision to support religious education is made by the individual, not by the State."[193] Moreover, no "significant portion of the aid expended under the Washington program . . . will *end up flowing* to religious education."[194] The establishment clause is therefore not breached.

Several justices felt obliged to submit concurring opinions. Justice White briefly repeated his view that "the Court's decisions finding constitutional violations where a state provides aid to private schools or their students misconstrue the Establishment Clause and disserve the public interest."[195] Justice O'Connor concurred in most of the Court's opinion, but wanted to point out that "[n]o reasonable observer is likely to draw from the facts before us an inference that the state itself is endorsing a religious practice or belief."[196] And Justice Powell, joined by Justice Rehnquist and Chief Justice Burger, issued a defense of the Court's decision in the *Mueller v. Allen* case lest Justice Marshall's opinion "mislead courts and litigants by suggesting that *Mueller* is somehow inapplicable to cases such as this one."[197] Rather, under *Mueller*, state programs that are "wholly neutral in offering educational assistance to a class defined without reference to religion do not violate the second part of the [*Lemon*] test, because an aid to religion results from the private choices of individual beneficiaries."[198] It was, therefore, wrong for the Washington court to analyze the case as if the vocational rehabilitation assistance had been directed solely at the petitioner's situation rather than seeing it as a broad-based program allowing individuals to choose the type of education they would receive.

In June of 1987, the Supreme Court handed down its decision in *Edwards v. Aguillard* declaring unconstitutional Louisiana's Balanced Treatment for Creation-Science and Evolution-Science in Public School Instruction Act.[199] Under this legislation, any school teaching either evolution or creationism must also teach the other. Justice Brennan delivered the Court's opinion, and he began with the *Lemon* test, pointing out that it had "been applied in all cases since its adoption in 1971, except in *Marsh v. Chambers* [where the] Court based its conclusion . . . on the historical acceptance of the practice."[200] For Brennan, who filed a strident dissent in *Marsh*, that case is inapposite because "[s]uch a historical approach is not useful in determining the proper roles of church and state in public schools, since free public education was virtually nonexistent at the time the Constitution was adopted."[201]

After taking note of the impressionability of elementary and secondary school students whose attendance is "involuntary," Justice Brennan first addressed the law's purpose, concluding that instead of the stated purpose of promoting academic freedom, the act "has the distinctly different purpose of discrediting evolution by counterbalancing its teaching at every turn with the teaching of creation science."[202] And, based on Justice Brennan's review of the legislative history, creation science "as contemplated by the legislature . . . embodies the religious belief that a supernatural creator was responsible for the creation of humankind."[203] The act was, therefore, unconstitutional under the establishment clause "because it seeks to employ the symbolic and financial support of government to achieve a religious purpose."[204]

In a concurring opinion Justice Powell, joined by Justice O'Connor, invoked the *Lemon* test but emphasized that the religious purpose of a law must "predominate" to render the act unconstitutional.[205] Also finding an impermissibly religious purpose, Justice Powell went on to reaffirm the Court's statements to the effect that instruction about religion, such as comparative religion, is consistent with the establishment clause.[206]

Justice Scalia, joined by the chief justice, submitted in dissent a harsh criticism of the "purpose" prong of the *Lemon* test. Noting with pragmatic honesty the many forces that may motivate legislators to vote for particular bills—from sincere concern for a law's merits to a desire to curry favor with the governor or pay back the bill's sponsor for some previous accommodation—Justice Scalia concluded that the "purpose" portion of the *Lemon* test "is defensible . . . only if the text of the Establishment Clause demands it," which he concluded, it does not.[207] Thus, since the purpose test "has no basis in the language or history of the [first] amendment," Justice Scalia proposed that it be abandoned altogether.[208]

A week after rendering the *Aguillard* decision, the Court faced a challenge under the establishment clause to a section of Title VII of the Civil Rights Act of 1964. In *Corporation of the Presiding Bishop v. Amos* (1987), the Court, in a rare unanimous decision, upheld the section of the Civil Rights Act that exempts religious organizations from Title VII's prohibitions on religious discrimination in employment. This case involved an employee of a nonprofit gymnasium run by a religious organization who was dismissed as a building engineer for failing to maintain membership in the Mormon church.[209] Justice White wrote the Court's opinion, and despite his regular appeals for a new approach to the establishment clause, he pursued a traditional *Lemon* test analysis. He concurred with the trial court that the law's secular purpose was "to minimize governmental 'interfer[ences] with the decision-making process in religions.' "[210] In analyzing the "effect" test, Justice White commented that a "law is not unconstitutional simply because it *allows* churches to advance religion, which is their very purpose," rather, for a "law to have forbidden 'effects' under *Lemon*, it must be fair to say that the *government itself* has advanced religion through its activities and influence."[211] In this case, Justice White found no such impermissible advancement of religion, nor did he see any problem under the entanglement test.

Justice Brennan, joined by Justice Marshall, submitted a concurring opinion emphasizing that the challenged exemption withstood constitutional challenge because it was a nonprofit organization. In Justice Brennan's view, "[R]eligious organizations should be able to discriminate on the basis of religion *only* with respect to religious activities, so that a determination should be made in each case whether an activity is religious or secular."[212]

Justice O'Connor also issued a concurring opinion in which she not only echoed Justice Brennan's distinction between for-profit and nonprofit entities, but she again expressed dissatisfaction with the *Lemon* test and renewed her appeal for an "endorsement" inquiry. To apply the endorsement test, Justice O'Connor asserted that "the relevant issue is how it would be perceived by an objective observer, acquainted with the text, legislative history, and implementation of the statute."[213]

The next case under the establishment clause brought the Court into the controversial realm of sex education and family planning. In response to a variety of social problems related to teenage pregnancy and childbirth, Congress adopted the Adolescent Family Life Act to provide grants to "public or nonprofit private organizations or agencies for services and research in the area of premarital adolescent sexual relations and pregnancy."[214] Among other things, the act required grant applications to state "how they will involve other organizations, including religious organizations," in funded programs.[215] Moreover, religious organizations were eligible to receive federal funds. In *Bowen v. Kendrick* (1988), a number of plaintiffs, including several members of the clergy and the American Jewish Congress, sought to have the act invalidated as an unconstitutional establishment of religion.

Chief Justice Rehnquist delivered the Court's majority opinion holding that the act is not unconstitutional on its face. Applying the three-part *Lemon* test (of which Justice Rehnquist appeared to approve at least with respect to facial challenges to a statute), the chief justice concluded that Congress had a legitimate secular purpose in reducing or eliminating the social problems caused by teenage pregnancy. The primary effect inquiry was admittedly more difficult, according to Justice Rehnquist, and ultimately the case was remanded for further consideration of how the act had been applied. But on its face, the act did not have the primary effect of advancing religion because Congress may constitutionally decide that religious organizations, as well as nonreligious charitable organizations, can help solve the problems addressed by the act.[216] To finance this aid, Congress may also provide federal funds to religious organizations since nothing in the act suggested that "a significant proportion of the federal funds will be disbursed to 'pervasively sectarian' institutions."[217] (Justices Kennedy and Scalia, in a concurring opinion, observed that even if the aid flowed to a pervasively sectarian institution, the act would still withstand constitutional challenge.) Finally, under the entanglement test, Justice Rehnquist observed that "this case presents us with yet another 'Catch–22' argument: the very supervision of the aid to assure that it does not further religion renders the statute invalid."[218] Not surprisingly, he concluded that the required amount of monitoring will not bring about an excessive entanglement between government and religion.

Justice Blackmun, joined by Justices Brennan, Marshall, and Stevens, wrote a strongly worded dissent arguing that the majority deviated sharply from the Court's parochial school aid cases. Among other things, Justice Blackmun observed that the act placed no restrictions on how funds could be used and that federal funds had actually been used to support clearly sectarian religious activity.[219]

In *Hernandez v. Commissioner of Internal Revenue* (1989), the Court considered the deductibility of payments made to the Church of Scientology in return for "auditing" and "training" courses offered by the church. The purpose of these courses, according to Scientologist doctrine, was to increase the adherents' awareness of their spirituality, and proceeds from the "fixed donations" set for the courses represented the Church of Scientology's principal revenue source. The petitioners in this case had deducted these fixed donations as charitable contributions under Section 170 of the Internal Revenue Code, but the deductions were disallowed by the Internal Revenue Service (the "Service") because the payments "were part of a quintessential quid pro quo exchange: in return for their money, petitioners received an identifiable benefit, namely, auditing and training sessions."[220] The petitioners argued that this traditional quid pro quo analysis was inconsistent with the establishment clause, among other things. They based this claim on two grounds: First, that this approach discriminated against religions that raised funds by prescribing charges for certain services, and second, that Section 170 of the Internal Revenue Code created an excessive governmental entanglement with religion because it requires the Service to supervise religious beliefs and practices and to place a value on religious services.[221]

In an opinion by Justice Marshall (joined by Rehnquist, White, Blackmun, and Stevens—with Justices Brennan and Kennedy not taking part in the case), the Court held that the payments were not deductible as charitable contributions. With respect to the establishment clause, Justice Marshall pointed to *Larson v. Valente* for the proper "analytic framework." Under *Larson*, "when it is claimed that a denominational preference exists, the initial inquiry is whether the law facially differentiates among religions. If no such facial preference exists, we proceed to apply the customary three-pronged [*Lemon*] test."[222] According to Justice Marshall, Section 170 neither shows facial discrimination nor violates any of the *Lemon* tests. Its purpose is not directed at religion or Scientology; it involves no advancement or inhibition of religion even though it imposed a "disparate burden on those . . . groups that rely on sales of commodities or services as a means of fundraising." And the "routine regulatory interaction which involves no inquiries into religious doctrine" created no excessive entanglement between government and religion.[223]

Not all of the justices agreed with Justice Marshall. In a dissenting opinion Justice O'Connor, joined by Justice Scalia, concluded that the Service's application of Section 170 violated the establishment clause. Its allowance of deductions for pew rents, entrance tickets for Holy Day services, and the like was inconsistent with the disallowance of the Scientologists' payments. This "differential application" is based on "constitutionally impermissible differences drawn by the Government among religions. . . . This the Government may not do."[224]

The next establishment clause case found the Court still divided, and Justice Brennan's opinion, which announced the judgment, commanded only the votes of Justices Marshall and Stevens. In *Texas Monthly v. Bullock* (1989), the Justices considered a Texas sales tax exemption for "[p]eriodicals that are published or distributed by a religious faith and that consist wholly of writings promulgating the teaching of the faith and books that consist wholly of writings sacred to a religious faith."[225] Noting that prior cases upholding certain aid to religion "emphasized that the benefits . . . flowed to a large number of nonreligious groups as well," Justice Brennan concluded that the tax exemption violated the establishment clause because it was available only to religious organizations and not to a variety of charitable organizations as the real property tax exemption upheld years earlier in *Walz* had been.[226]

Had Justice Brennan's opinion stopped at this point, he probably would have enlisted at least two more justices to sign on to his opinion. But he went on to argue that the First Amendment's free exercise clause would not prohibit a state from "imposing a general sales tax on religious publications."[227] Justice Blackmun's concurring opinion, in which Justice O'Connor joined, took issue with "Justice Brennan's opinion [which] would resolve the tension between the Free Exercise and Establishment Clause values simply by subordinating the Free Exercise value, even, it seems to me, at the expense of longstanding precedents."[228] This theme was also picked up by Justice Scalia in his dissenting opinion (joined by the chief justice and Justice Kennedy), which called Brennan's approach a "judicial demolition project" of numerous precedents, such as *Walz* as well as forty-five analogous state laws.[229]

One of the most publicized Supreme Court cases of 1989 was *Webster v. Reproductive Health Services*, in which the justices considered the continuing vitality of the historic *Roe v. Wade* decision on constitutional protection for abortion. The Court, which upheld a Missouri statute regulating abortion without overturning *Roe v. Wade*, generally avoided issues of religion except for Justice Stevens, who, in his concurring and dissenting opinion, concluded that "the absence of any secular purpose for the legislative declarations that life begins at conception . . . makes [that] portion . . . invalid under the Establishment Clause."[230] This conclusion rests not on any coincidence with religious tenets or religious motivations of the legislators, but because the law's declarations "serve . . . no identifiable secular purpose."[231] Justice Stevens then described at some length the views of Thomas Aquinas on abortion and placed the burden on the state to show why it has a secular interest in the first forty days of pregnancy.

In *County of Allegheny v. American Civil Liberties Union*, the Court heard another crèche case, thus bringing the nine justices to the scene of Jesus' birth more often than the Magi. For years, the city of Pittsburgh had erected holiday displays during the Christmas season. In one, a crèche was set up by a Roman Catholic group on the grand staircase of the county courthouse, and in the other a Chanukah menorah stood next to a Christmas tree and a "Statue of Liberty" plaque outside the city-county building. The justices issued a set of remarkable opinions, with the judgment of thc Court—condemning the crèche display but permitting the menorah—announced by Justice Blackmun. This opinion, however, only represented a majority of the Court for part of the discussion. In it, Justice Blackmun summarized the numerous approaches the Court had taken to the establishment clause, ultimately concluding that the "Establishment Clause, at the very least, prohibits government from appearing to take a position on questions of religious belief or from 'making adherence to a religion relevant in any way to a person's standing in the political community.' "[232] This leads to the conclusion, according to Justice Blackmun, who, at that point was speaking for five of the justices, that the Court's decisions in this case and *Lynch* could be reconciled on the grounds that "government may celebrate Christmas in some manner and form, but not in a way that endorses Christian doctrine."[233] Thus the crèche displayed in *Lynch* was permissible because there were enough reindeer and related nonreligious elements to distract from the crèche's religious theme. In this case, however, the crèche's message of "Glory to God for the birth of Jesus Christ"[234] was unencumbered by Santa's elves or the other symbols of the holiday season that somehow transform a religious Holy Day into a secular holiday.

Although the Court did not specify the ratio of elves to angels required to withstand an establishment clause challenge, its treatment of the menorah may provide some guidance. According to Justice Blackmun—who garnered no support from other justices for this part of his opinion—the menorah could be displayed without violating the Constitution because it stood with a Christmas tree and a sign proclaiming freedom. The presence of the tree "as the preeminent secular symbol of the Christmas holiday season serves to emphasize the secular components of the message . . . of an accompanying holiday display, including the Chanukah menorah."[235]

Justice O'Connor's concurring opinion supported the Court's judgment on both the crèche and the menorah, and it is perhaps most noteworthy for its vigorous defense of the endorsement test the justice has developed in earlier cases. This defense, in the face of a strident attack by Justice Kennedy, was joined by Justices Brennan and Stevens. Justice Blackmun wrote a separate defense of the endorsement approach in his opinion. Thus, Justice O'Connor's test appears to have won over four of the nine justices, although its promise of relief from the unwieldy three-part *Lemon* test may have diminished. At the very end of her opinion, Justice O'Connor concluded that the "combined holiday display had neither the purpose nor the effect of endorsing religion."[236] All she needs to do is ask whether the challenged activity creates an entanglement between religion and government leading to an endorsement of religion and she will have completed the full circle back to the *Lemon* test.

Justice Brennan, who would have disallowed both the crèche and the menorah as showing governmental favoritism towards religion, called Justice Blackmun's contextual approach to the menorah "more like an exam in Art 101 than an inquiry into constitutional law."[237] And Justice Kennedy, writing for Chief Justice Rehnquist and Justices White and Scalia, blasted the majority's disallowance of the crèche as "bizarre," Justice O'Connor's endorsement test as "flawed in its fundamentals and unworkable," and Justice Blackmun's opinion as "an Orwellian rewriting of history" (for which Blackmun dubbed Kennedy's dissenting opinion "Orwellian newspeak"). Needless to say, the justices remain sharply divided on the establishment clause.

For Justice Kennedy and his colleagues, the majority's disallowance of the crèche represented "an unjustified hostility toward religion, a hostility inconsistent with our history and our precedents."[238] Suggesting that "[s]ubstantial revision of our Establishment Clause doctrine may be in order," Kennedy asserted that the crèche would pass muster even under the *Lemon* test.[239] Existing precedents disclose, according to Justice Kennedy, only "two limiting principles" dividing permissible accommodations of religion and unconstitutional establishments: "[G]overnment may not coerce anyone to support or participate in any religion or its exercise; and it may not, in the guise of avoidance hostility or callous indifference, give direct benefits to religion in such a degree that it in fact 'establishes a [state] religion or religious faith, or tends to do so' [citing *Lynch*]."[240]

Despite these acrimonious opinions, just a few months later mail-order sales of books, tapes, and other religious articles by the Jimmy Swaggart Ministries brought the Court to a rare unanimous decision. The state of California assessed sales tax with respect to these transactions, and the ministries asserted, among other things, that the imposition of sales tax violated the establishment clause by creating an excessive entanglement between government and religion. This alleged entanglement resulted from the lengthy inspection of the Ministries' books, audits, administrative proceedings, and the like. Without clearly taking a position on the vitality of the three-part test, Justice O'Connor's opinion easily concluded that the state's activity in collecting taxes did not create an excessive entanglement, particularly because the tax "does not require the state to inquire into the religious content of the items sold or the religious motivation for selling or purchasing the items, because the materials are subject to tax regardless of content or motive."[241]

In 1990, the Court again returned to the public schools to consider the constitutionality of student religious groups meeting during after-school hours. In *Board of Education of the Westside Community Schools v. Mergens*, the Supreme Court scrutinized the Equal Access Act adopted by Congress forbidding any secondary school receiving federal funds "and which has a limited open forum to deny equal access or a fair opportunity to, or discriminate against, any students who wish to conduct a meeting within that limited open forum on the basis of the religious, political, philosophical, or other content of the speech at such meetings."[242] Originally developed in the *Widmar* case (which involved a public university rather than a secondary school), a "limited open forum" was found by the Court to exist when a school "permits one or more 'noncurriculum related student groups' to meet on campus before or after classes."[243]

Justice O'Connor announced the Court's judgment finding the act to be constitutional under the establishment clause, but only the chief justice and Justices White and Blackmun joined her in this approach. Following the approach used in *Widmar*, which involved the use of the *Lemon* tests, Justice O'Connor concluded that the act's protection of "political, philosophical, or other" speech, in addition to religious speech, demonstrated a secular purpose. The act also passed muster under the "primary effect" inquiry because "there is a crucial difference between government speech endorsing religion, which the Establishment Clause forbids, and private speech endorsing religion, which the Free Speech and Free Exercise Clauses protect."[244] In Justice O'Connor's opinion, "[S]econdary school students are mature enough and are likely to understand that a school does not endorse or support student speech that it merely permits on a nondiscriminatory basis."[245] This is especially true in light of the act's limitation on the participation by school officials in student religious groups, which also led to Justice O'Connor's conclusion that the Equal Access Act would not create an excessive entanglement between government and religion.[246]

Justice Kennedy (joined by Justice Scalia) concurred in the judgment, but made a point of taking a much more accommodationist position than Justice O'Connor. For Justice Kennedy, an accommodation of religion by the schools is permissible unless it "violates either one of two principles. The first is that the government cannot 'give direct benefits to religion in such a degree that it in fact establishes a [state] religion or religious faith, or tends to do so.' . . . The second . . . is that the government cannot coerce any student to participate in a religious activity."[247] Referring to his concurring opinion in *County of Allegheny*, Justice Kennedy reiterated that the endorsement test "may result in neutrality in name but hostility in fact when the question is the government's proper relation to those who express some religious preference."[248]

In a relatively rare event in establishment clause cases, Justices Marshall and Brennan concurred that the act should survive constitutional scrutiny, but Justice Marshall's concurring opinion sought to emphasize the need for public secondary schools to take steps to avoid the appearance of endorsing religion. In particular, Justice Marshall urged that schools have "a wide range of ideological clubs [so that] students [will] reasonably understand the school [does not] endorse all the groups' divergent and contradictory views."[249] If, however, the religious group is the only "advocacy-oriented group . . . or one of a limited number" there will be the risk of an endorsement of that activity.[250]

Justice Stevens filed a dissenting opinion focusing on whether the high school had, in fact, established the kind of limited open forum protected under the free speech clause in *Widmar*. He concluded that it had not done so, and as a result the act's provisions requiring equal access would not apply and should not be reviewed under the establishment clause.[251]

This set of opinions—in which once again no justice commanded the votes of a majority of the Court—brings to a characteristically confusing close the history of the establishment clause before the United States Supreme Court, at least to the time of this writing. In the last couple of years, however, numerous events have taken place that appear to be setting the stage for a major reworking of establishment clause doctrine. It is impossible to predict whether there will be a complete swing to the strongly accommodationist views often displayed by Justices Rehnquist, Kennedy, and Scalia, or to the more moderate position staked out by Justice O'Connor, but there is no question that the Court will search for—and find—a new approach. We must, accordingly, reexamine with particular rigor the history and background of the establishment clause's adoption and the complex relationship of church and state in our country to elucidate a constitutional doctrine that will bring clarity and consistency to an area fraught with confusion and complexity.

NOTES

1. Lewis Carroll, "Through the Looking Glass," in Philip C. Blackburn and Lionel White, eds., *Logical Nonsense: The Works of Lewis Carroll* (New York: G. P. Putnam's Sons, 1934), p. 205.

2. Cranch 137, 2 L.Ed. 60 (1803). The Court reemphasized this position more recently in Cooper v. Aaron, 358 U.S. 1 (1958), saying, "[*Marbury v. Madison*] declared the basic principle that the federal judiciary is supreme in the exposition of the law of the Constitution, and that principle has ever since been respected by this Court and the Country as a permanent and indispensable feature of our Constitutional system." This principle has not always been popular in

the executive branch. Several presidents have spoken against it, Jefferson arguing that "to consider the judges as the ultimate arbiters of all constitutional questions [is] a very dangerous doctrine indeed, and one which would place us under the despotism of an oligarchy." Paul Leicester Ford, ed., *The Writings of Thomas Jefferson*, vol. 10, p. 160 (letter to William C. Jarvis, September, 28, 1820) (New York: G. P. Putnam, 1892–99).

3. Carroll, "Through the Looking Glass," p. 205.

4. Clinton Rossiter, ed., *The Federalist Papers* (New York: New American Library, 1961), p. 229 (Federalist No. 37).

5. For more along this line, see Max Lerner, "The Constitution and the Court as Symbols," 46 *Yale Law Journal* 1290 (1937); Sanford Levinson, *Constitutional Faith* (Princeton, N.J.: Princeton University Press, 1988); and Harold J. Berman, *The Interaction of Law and Religion* (Nashville: Abingdon, 1975).

6. Reynolds v. United States, 98 U.S. 145 (1879).

7. Ibid. at 162.

8. Ibid. at 163.

9. Ibid.

10. Ibid.

11. Ibid.

12. Ibid.

13. Ibid. at 164.

14. Ibid.

15. Ibid. at 165.

16. Davis v. Beason, 133 U.S. 333 (1890).

17. Ibid. at 345. See also Wooley v. Watkins, 2 Idaho 555, 22 Pac. 102 (1889) holding that a statute making ineligible to vote or hold public office any persons teaching or practicing polygamy or belonging to an organization that does so is not an invasion of religious liberty or the imposition of a religious test for public office.

18. 133 U.S. at 345.

19. Church of Jesus Christ of Latter-Day Saints v. United States, 136 U.S. 1 (1890).

20. See James D. Richardson, *Messages and Papers of the Presidents* (New York: Bureau of National Literature, 1897), Proclamation of Benjamin Harrison, January 4, 1893, vol. 12, pp. 5803–4, and Proclamation of Grover Cleveland, September 25, 1894, vol. 12, pp. 5942–43.

21. Bradfield v. Roberts, 175 U.S. 291 (1899).

22. Ibid. at 293.

23. Ibid. at 298–99.

24. Quick Bear v. Leupp, 210 U.S. 50 (1908).

25. Ibid. at 81.

26. Ibid.

27. Ibid. at 82.

28. Everson v. Board of Education, 330 U.S. 1 (1947), reh. denied, 330 U.S. 855 (1947).

29. Cantwell v. Connecticut, 310 U.S. 296 (1940). A similar case arose in the Supreme Court before *Cantwell* involving a state practice of furnishing textbooks on secular subjects to religious schools. In that case, the establishment clause was not discussed because the plaintiffs had only claimed that the textbook program

was the taking of public resources for private use. The program was upheld by the Court, and the defendants in *Everson* hoped that the earlier case would be dispositive. See Cochran v. Louisiana State Board of Education, 281 U.S. 370 (1930).

30. 330 U.S. at 11.
31. Ibid.
32. Ibid. at 13.
33. Ibid. at 15–16.
34. Ibid.
35. Ibid. at 18.
36. Ibid.
37. Ibid. at 19.
38. Ibid. at 33–34.
39. 330 U.S. at 37. Justice Rutledge attached a copy of the "Memorial and Remonstrance" as an appendix to his opinion.
40. Madison did not believe that the federal government had any power to support or hinder religion, and, therefore, was not concerned about the lack of provisions dealing with religion in the Constitution. See William T. Hutchison et al., eds., *The Papers of James Madison*, 13 vol. (Chicago: University of Chicago Press, 1962–1969), vol. 2, pp. 297–98.
41. 330 U.S. at 39.
42. Illinois ex rel. McCollum v. Board of Education, 333 U.S. 203 (1948).
43. Ibid. at 209.
44. Ibid. at 210.
45. Ibid. at 215.
46. Ibid. at 216–17.
47. Ibid. at 227.
48. Ibid. at 244.
49. Ibid.
50. Ibid. at 247.
51. Ibid. at 256.
52. Ibid. at 238.
53. Zorach v. Clauson, 343 U.S. 306 (1951).
54. Ibid. at 315.
55. Ibid. at 312–13.
56. Ibid. at 313–14.
57. McGowan v. Maryland, 366 U.S. 420 (1961); Gallagher v. Crown Kosher Super Market of Massachusetts, 366 U.S. 617 (1961); Two Guys from Harrison-Allentown, Inc. v. McGinley, 366 U.S. 582 (1961); Braunfield v. Brown, 366 U.S. 599 (1961).
58. 366 U.S. at 431. The Court noted that the original English Sunday legislation was clearly "in aid of the established church," as were the colonial laws beginning in America in the seventeenth century: "For example, a 1629 Massachusetts Bay instruction began, 'And to the end of the Sabbath may be celebrated in a religious manner.' " 366 U.S. at 433.
59. For Supreme Court *dicta* in support of this position see, for example, Soon Hing v. Crowley, 113 U.S. 703 (1885), in which the Court said, "Laws setting aside Sunday as a day of rest are upheld, not from any right of the Government to legislate for the promotion of religious observances, but from its right to protect

all persons from the physical and moral debasement which comes from uninterrupted labor." 113 U.S. at 710.

60. 366 U.S. at 437.

61. Ibid. at 422.

62. Ibid.

63. Ibid. at 445.

64. Torcaso v. Watkins, 367 U.S. 488 (1961).

65. Ibid. at 494.

66. Engel v. Vitale, 370 U.S. 421 (1962).

67. Ibid. at 430–31.

68. Ibid. at 425, 8 L.Ed. 2d at 605.

69. Ibid. at 428–29.

70. Ibid. at 435 (note 21).

71. Ibid. at 450.

72. School District of Abington Township v. Schempp, 374 U.S. 203 (1963).

73. 374 U.S. at 214, citing Williams's statement: "I affirm that all the liberty of conscience I ever pleaded for, turns upon these two hinges, that none of the Papists, protestants, Jews or Turks be forced to come to the ship's prayers or worship, nor compelled from their own particular prayers or worship, if they practice any" (note 6).

74. Ibid. at 222.

75. Ibid. at 225.

76. Ibid.

77. Ibid. at 227 et seq. See also Justice Douglas, concurring opinion in Engel v. Vitale, 370 U.S. at 437.

78. 374 U.S. at 306.

79. Ibid. at 202.

80. Ibid. at 310. Justice Stewart enthusiastically supported the *Cantwell* holding that the Fourteenth Amendment fully embraces the First Amendment's guarantee of the free exercise of religion, but was less ebullient in agreeing that "the Fourteenth Amendment has somehow absorbed the Establishment Clause" (344 U.S. at 310).

81. Ibid. at 237–38.

82. Ibid. at 241.

83. Ibid.

84. Ibid. at 300–4.

85. For the quotations, see Philip B. Kurland, "The School Prayer Cases," in Dallin H. Oaks, ed., *The Wall Between Church and State* (Chicago and London: University of Chicago Press, 1963), pp. 142–146.

86. The version of the early sixties was more verbose. Introduced by Congressman Frank Becker and fifty-eight of his colleagues, the proposal read: "Section 1. Nothing in this Constitution shall be deemed to prohibit the offering, reading from, or listening to prayers or biblical scriptures, if participation therein is on a voluntary basis, in any governmental or public school, institution, or place. Section 2. Nothing in this Constitution shall be deemed to prohibit making reference to belief in, reliance upon, or invoking the aid of God or a Supreme Being in any governmental or public document, proceeding, activity, ceremony, school, institution, or place, or upon any coinage, currency, or obligation of the United States.

Section 3. Nothing in this article shall constitute an establishment of religion." For further discussion of the Sturm und Drang attending this proposal, see Joseph A. Fisher, "The Becker Amendment: A Constitutional Trojan Horse," *Journal of Church and State* 11, no. 3 (Autumn 1969), pp. 427–55; U.S. Congress, Senate, Committee on the Judiciary, *Prayers in Public Schools and Other Matters* 87th Cong. 2nd Sess. 1962 (Washington, D.C.: Government Printing Office, 1963); and U.S. Congress, House of Representatives, Committee on the Judiciary, *School Prayers*, 88th Cong. 2nd Sess., 1964 (Washington, D.C.: Government Printing Office, 1965).

87. See, for example, Wallace v. Jaffree, 86 L.Ed. 2d 29 (1985), and Kenneth M. Dolbeare and Philip E. Hammond, *The School Prayer Decisions: From Court Policy to Local Practice* (Chicago: University of Chicago Press, 1971).

88. Epperson v. Arkansas, 393 U.S. 97 (1968).

89. Scopes v. State, 154 Tenn. 105, 289 S.W. 363 (1927). Scopes, a public school teacher, was originally convicted and fined, but his conviction was overturned on a technicality by the Tennessee Supreme Court. A majority of the court found the law to be constitutional.

90. For more on the *Scopes* trial, see Irving Stone, *Clarence Darrow for the Defense* (New York: Bantam Books, 1941) and the books cited in Andrew D. Bing, "Evolution, Creationism and the Religion Clauses," *Albany Law Review* 46, no. 3 (Spring 1982), p. 897, note 5. On the modern creationism-evolution controversy see, for example, Edward J. Larson, *Trial and Error: The American Controversy Over Creation and Evolution* (New York: Oxford University Press, 1985); Wendell Bird, "Freedom of Religion and Science Instruction in Public Schools," *Yale Law Journal* 87 (1978) pp. 515–70; and Bing, above.

91. 393 U.S. 97, 109 (1968). For what it is worth, a poll conducted for the *ABA Journal* found that sixty-three percent of lawyers surveyed believed that the teaching of creationism in public schools does not violate the establishment clause. Paul Reidinger, "Creationism and the First Amendment," *ABA Journal* (January 1, 1987), p. 35.

92. Board of Education v. Allen, 392 U.S. 236.

93. Ralph M. Silberman, "Supreme Court's Views Regarding State Aid to Sectarian Schools under Establishment and Freedom of Religion Clauses of United States Constitution," 63 L.Ed. 2d 804, 813. This annotation contains a useful discussion of the parochial school aid cases up to 1980.

94. Walz v. Tax Commission, 397 U.S. 664, 668 (1970).

95. Ibid. at 669.

96. Ibid. at 673.

97. Ibid. at 674.

98. Ibid.

99. Ibid. at 675–76, citing New York Trust Co. v. Eisner, 256 U.S. 345, 349 (1921). Justice Brennan concurred in this approach, arguing, "Rarely if ever has this Court considered the constitutionality of a practice for which the historical support is so overwhelming." 397 U.S., at 681 (concurring opinion).

100. Ibid. at 695 (concurring opinion).

101. See Paul Freund, "Public Aid to Parochial Schools," 82 *Harvard Law Review* 1680 (1969). Although Freund offered no historical support for his comment, it has been traced by other scholars to Madison's *Federalist No. 10*, in which

Madison cautions against the possible adverse effects on government caused by factions which he defines as a "number of citizens, whether amounting to a majority or minority of the whole, who are united and actuated by some common impulse or passion, or of interests adverse to the rights of other citizens, or to the permanent and aggregate interests of the community." See A. E. Dick Howard, "Up Against the Wall: The Uneasy Separation of Church and State," in *Church, State and Politics* (Washington, D.C.: Roscoe Pound–American Trial Lawyers Foundation), p. 23. See also Edward M. Gaffney, Jr., "Political Divisiveness along Religious Lines: The Entanglement of the Court in Sloppy History and Bad Public Policy," 24 *St. Louis Law Review* 205 (1980).

102. Justice Douglas's dissenting opinion can be found at 397 U.S. at 700–727.

103. Lemon v. Kurtzman, 403 U.S. 602, 612 (1971).

104. Ibid. at 612 (emphasis in the original).

105. Ibid. at 612–13.

106. Ibid. at 613–14.

107. Ibid. at 617.

108. Ibid.

109. Ibid. at 622.

110. Justice Douglas, concurring opinion is at 403 U.S. at 625–42.

111. Ibid. at 642 (concurring opinion).

112. Ibid. at 643 (concurring opinion).

113. Ibid. at 658 (concurring opinion).

114. Tilton v. Richardson, 403 U.S. 672 (1971).

115. See Walz v. Tax Commission, 397 U.S. 664, 668 (1970).

116. Compare Everson with Wolman v. Walter, 433 U.S. 349 (1975).

117. Compare Board of Education v. Allen, with Meek v. Pittenger, 421 U.S. 349 (1975).

118. See Nathan Lewin, "Dissentangling Myth from Reality," *Journal of Law and Education* 3 (1974), pp. 107–8; Howard, "Up Against the Wall," p. 21; and Philip R. Moots and Edward M. Gaffrey, Jr., *Church and Campus: Legal Issues in Religiously Affiliated Education* (Notre Dame, Ind.: University of Notre Dame Press, 1979).

119. Levitt v. Committee for Public Education and Religious Liberty ("PEARL"), Anderson v. PEARL, Cathedral Academy v. PEARL, 413 U.S. 472 (1973); Hunt v. McNair, 413 U.S. 734 (1973); PEARL v. Nyquist, Anderson v. PEARL, Nyquist v. PEARL, Cherry v. PEARL, 413 U.S. 756 (1973); Sloan v. Lemon, Crouter v. Lemon, 413 U.S. 825 (1973).

120. Committee for Public Education v. Nyquist, 413 U.S. 756, 760 (1973). In a later footnote, Justice Powell again harkened back to "Virginia's experience [which] constitutes one of the greatest chapters in the history of this country's adoption of the essentially revolutionary notion of separation between Church and State." 413 U.S. at 769 note 28.

121. Ibid. at 761.

122. Ibid. at 771.

123. Ibid. at 779–80.

124. Ibid. at 794.

125. Ibid. at 797–98.

126. Ibid. at 799 (concurring and dissenting opinions).

127. Ibid. at 820 (dissenting opinion).

128. Edward S. Corwin, "The Supreme Court as National School Board," *Law and Contemporary Problems* 14 (1949), pp. 3–22. Citing Justice Jackson, Corwin wrote in opposition to the *McCollum* decision, "[T]he Court would act wisely to make it clear at the first opportunity that it does not aspire to become . . . 'a super board of education for every school district in the nation' " (p. 22).

129. Stone v. Graham, 449 U.S. 39 (1980).

130. Ibid. at 40–41.

131. Title VIII of Public Law 98–377.

132. Widmar v. Vincent, 454 U.S. 263 (1981).

133. Ibid. at 273.

134. Larson v. Valente, 456 U.S. 228 (1982).

135. Ibid. at 244.

136. Ibid. at 247.

137. Ibid. at 252.

138. Ibid. at 253.

139. Ibid. at 254.

140. Ibid. at 260.

141. Larkin v. Grendel's Den, 459 U.S. 116 (1982).

142. Ibid. at 125–26.

143. Ibid. at 127. Although Justice Burger commanded the votes of virtually all the justices in *Grendel's Den*, he also drew the ire of Justice Rehnquist who opined that "silly cases," like hard ones, make bad law. As he put it: "The aim of [the Court's] effort is to prove that a quite sensible Massachusetts liquor zoning law is apparently some sort of sinister religious attack on secular government reminiscent of St. Bartholomew's Night. Being unpersuaded, I dissent." 459 U.S. at 128. Justice Rehnquist concluded by pointing out that the "heavy First Amendment artillery that the Court fires at this sensible and unobjectionable Massachusetts statute is both unnecessary and unavailing." 459 U.S. at 130.

144. Marsh v. Chambers, 463 U.S. 783 (1983).

145. Ibid. at 3335–36.

146. Ibid. at 3336.

147. Ibid. at 796.

148. Ibid. at 802 (emphasis in the original).

149. Ibid. at 804.

150. Ibid. at 812.

151. Ibid. at 816.

152. Ibid. at 817. Justice Brennan was equally unhappy with the argument that legislative prayer is merely a minimal violation of the Constitution, ranking perhaps with "In God We Trust" on coins. Prayer is "serious business—serious theological business and the state should not become involved with it."

153. Ibid.

154. Ibid.

155. Lynch v. Donnelly, 465 U.S. 668 (1984).

156. Ibid. at 673.

157. Ibid. at 674.

158. Ibid. at 679.

159. Ibid. at 681.

160. Ibid. at 683, citing Mueller v. Allen, 463 U.S. 388 (1983). Here, the controversial political divisiveness test appears destined for emeritus status at best, not a surprising result in light of the Court's difficulty in dealing with it. In her concurring opinion, Justice O'Connor also sought to drop the dubious divisiveness inquiry. 465 U.S. 686.

161. 465 U.S. 687 (concurring opinion).

162. Ibid.

163. Ibid.

164. Ibid. at 692.

165. Ibid. at 693.

166. Jaffree v. James, 554 F.Supp. 1130, 1131–32 (S.D.Ala. 1983). This case, which involved the statute, was severed from the case challenging the actual prayers, Jaffree v. Board of School Commissioners of Mobile County, 554 F.Supp. 1104 (S.D.Ala. 1983), rev'd, Jaffree v. Wallace, 705 F.2d 1526 (11th Cir. 1983), aff'd, Wallace v. Jaffree, 466 U.S. 924, 80 L.Ed. 2d 178, 104 S.Ct. 1704 (1984) and 86 L.Ed. 2d 29 (1985).

167. Jaffree v. James, 544 F.Supp. 727, 731 (S.D.Ala. 1982).

168. Jaffree v. James, 554 F.Supp. at 1132.

169. Jaffree v. Board of School Commissioners, 554 F.Supp. at 1117–18.

170. Wallace v. Jaffree, 86 L.Ed. 2d at 38 citing Wallace v. Jaffree, 466 U.S. 924 (1984).

171. 86 L.Ed. 2d at 38.

172. Ibid. at 54 (concurring opinion).

173. Ibid. at 61 (concurring opinion).

174. Ibid. at 62–65 (dissenting opinion).

175. Ibid. at 66 (dissenting opinion).

176. Ibid. at 71.

177. 86 L.Ed. 2d, pp. 71–74. Justice Rehnquist also elicited the support of nineteenth-century legal giants Justice Joseph Story ("Probably at the time of the adoption of the Constitution, and of the [First Amendment], the general if not the universal sentiment in America was, that Christianity ought to receive encouragement from the State so far as was not incompatible with the private rights of conscience and the freedom of religious worship.") and Thomas Cooley ("[T]he American constitutions contain no provisions which prohibit the authorities from such solemn recognition of a superintending Providence in public transactions and exercises as the general religious sentiment of mankind inspires."). 86 L.Ed. 2d, pp. 74–75.

178. Ibid., p. 75.

179. Estate of Thornton v. Caldor, 86 L.Ed. 2d 557 (1985).

180. Ibid., p. 563. The Court cited Learned Hand's "well articulated" statement of the "fundamental principle of the Religion Clauses . . . 'The First Amendment . . . gives no one the right to insist that in pursuit of their own interests others must conform their conduct to his own religious necessities.' Otten v. Baltimore & Ohio R.R. Co., 205 F. 2d 58, 61 (CA 2 1953)."

181. 86 L.Ed. 2d, p. 564.

182. 87 L.Ed. 2d 267 (1985).

183. Ibid. at 276–77. Justice Brennan again tried to shore up an apparently faltering three-part test, saying, "The Lemon test concentrates attention on the

issues—purpose, effect, entanglement—that determine whether a particular state action is an improper 'law respecting an establishment of religion.' We therefore reaffirm that state action alleged to violate the Establishment Clause should be measured against the Lemon criteria" (87 L.Ed. 2d at 276–77).

184. Ibid. at 278.

185. Justices Burger and O'Connor concurred as to the community program but voted to uphold the shared time program. Justices White and Rehnquist dissented, each calling for a revised approach to the establishment clause. 87 L.Ed. 2d at 287–89.

186. 87 L.Ed. 2d 290 (1985).

187. Ibid. at 300.

188. Ibid. at 305.

189. Ibid. at 304–12.

190. Witters v. Washington Department of Services for the Blind, 474 U.S. 481 (1986).

191. Ibid. at 483.

192. Ibid. at 485.

193. Ibid. at 488.

194. Ibid.

195. Ibid. at 489 (concurring opinion).

196. Ibid. at 493.

197. Ibid. at 490. In Mueller v. Allen, the Court upheld a tax deduction for the cost of tuition, textbooks, and school transportation.

198. Ibid. at 490–91.

199. 107 S.Ct. 2573 (1987).

200. Ibid., note 4.

201. Ibid.

202. Edwards v. Aguillard, 482 U.S. 582 (1987), p. 584.

203. Ibid. at 589.

204. Ibid. at 597.

205. Ibid. at 599.

206. Ibid. at 608–10. Justice White, concurring in the judgment, also submitted a brief opinion in which he concluded "that the two courts below are [not] so plainly wrong that they should be reversed." 482 U.S. at 610.

207. Ibid. at 639.

208. Ibid.

209. 197 S.Ct. 2862 (1987).

210. Ibid.

211. Ibid.

212. Ibid. at 642.

213. Ibid. at 645.

214. Bowen v. Kendrick, 101 L.Ed. 2d 520 (1988).

215. Ibid.

216. Ibid.

217. Ibid.

218. Ibid.

219. Ibid.

220. Hernandez v. Petitioner, 57 U.S.L.W. 4596 (1989).

221. Ibid. at 4597.
222. Ibid.
223. Ibid. at 4598.
224. Ibid. at 4602.
225. Texas Monthly v. Bullock, 103 L.Ed. 2d 1, 7 (1989).
226. Ibid. at 10–11.
227. Ibid. at 20.
228. Ibid. at 21.
229. Ibid. at 22.
230. Webster v. Reproductive Health Services, 106 L.Ed. 2d 410, 467 (1989).
231. Ibid.
232. County of Allegheny v. American Civil Liberties Union, 57 U.S.L.W. 5045, 5050, (1989) citing Justice O'Connor's concurring opinion in Lynch, 465 U.S. at 687.
233. Ibid. at 5052.
234. Ibid. at 5053.
235. Ibid. at 5057.
236. Ibid. at 5062.
237. Ibid. at 5064.
238. Ibid. at 5067.
239. Ibid.
240. Ibid. at 5068.
241. Ibid.
242. Board of Education of the Westside Community Schools v. Mergens, 1990 Lexis 1880, p. 8 (1990).
243. Ibid.
244. Ibid., p. 16.
245. Ibid.
246. Ibid., p. 17.
247. Ibid., p. 22.
248. Ibid.
249. Ibid., p. 25.
250. Ibid.
251. Ibid., p. 29.

2

THE QUEST FOR THE HISTORICAL ESTABLISHMENT CLAUSE

Taxonomists responsible for classifying all living things within the appropriate genus, species, phylum, and kingdom divide themselves into two groups—lumpers and splitters. As the names suggest, lumpers tend to look for ways to group various plants or animals together while their less-inclusive colleagues split the flora or fauna in question into many more categories. In the church-state taxonomy, I tend to be a lumper, dividing the spectrum of opinions on these issues into two kingdoms—the strict separationists and the accommodationists (into which I lump the "nonpreferentialists"). This method of classification may not do justice to the array of positions voiced in establishment clause cases, but it should suffice as a shorthand method of describing the principal participants in church-state debates.

The Supreme Court's reliance on the Founding Fathers' intent has made the establishment clause's background fertile ground for argumentative excavation, with strict separationists and accommodationists alike wielding their historical picks and shovels in search of support for their favored interpretations. The weight of current authority, both judicial and in terms of sheer volume, seems to lie with the strict separationists. Their number includes the vast majority of the Supreme Court justices in twentieth-century establishment clause cases as well as Pulitzer Prize-winning historian Leonard Levy and influential constitutional lawyer Leo Pfeffer. Their motto is "wall of separation," and their theme is perhaps most succinctly stated in Justice Black's opinion in *Everson v. Board of Education.*[1] There the establishment clause's roots are traced back to the "freedom-loving colonials," many of whom fled religious persecution in England and whose efforts on behalf of religious freedom climaxed in the enactment of Virginia's Bill for Establishing Religious Freedom. Finally, James Madison's drafting and sponsorship of the First Amendment imbued the amendment's sparse wording with the substance of the Virginia struggle in which he and Thomas Jefferson played such major parts. In this view, we must look to the writings of James Madison and Thomas Jefferson, especially Madison's "Memorial and Remonstrance" and the Bill for Establishing Religious Freedom, to guide (if not control) our interpretation of the establishment clause.[2] In so doing, we find Madison and Jefferson leading us to a strict separation of church and state that will not brook any support of religion by the government.

The opposing school of thought argues that the First Congress intended to allow government support of religion, at least as long as that support did not discriminate in favor of one particular religion. Supporters of this view arrive at this conclusion through one of two interpretive approaches. The first agrees with the strict separationists that we must look to Madison and Jefferson for the intent of the First Amendment, but then asserts that the Supreme Court has overlooked many important pieces of history. Madison, for example, was on the congressional committee that appointed a chaplain, he declared several national days of prayer and fasting during his presidency, and he sponsored Jefferson's Virginia bill for punishing Sabbath breakers; moreover, while president, Jefferson allowed federal support of religious missions to the Indians. On the day after the establishment clause was adopted, the entire First Congress passed a resolution in favor of a presidential proclamation declaring a national day of "Thanksgiving and Prayer." And so, concludes one recent book, "there is no support in the Congressional records that either the First Congress, which framed the First Amendment, or its principle author and sponsor, James Madison, intended that Amendment to create a state of complete independence between religion and government. In fact, the evidence in the public documents goes the other way."[3] In conclusion, these accommodationists argue, Madison and Jefferson would see nothing wrong with nondenominational prayers in the legislatures and the schools and similar governmental accommodations of religion.

The other group of accommodationists see the Madison-Jefferson connection as the fatal flaw in the Supreme Court's First Amendment jurisprudence. James Madison, they assert, did not draft the establishment clause. Madison's initial proposal was first changed by Samuel Livermore of New Hampshire and was later revised by Fisher Ames of Massachusetts, both of whom represented states interested in protecting their established churches from federal interference. In fact, Livermore's version prohibited

Congress from enacting any laws "touching religion," thus foreclosing Congress from either setting up its own established church or interfering with state establishments. (In other words, the Congress could neither effect nor affect a religious establishment.) Each state was thus left free to establish any policy it desired with respect to religion. Likewise, this group argues, the states should have the same freedom today, and the Supreme Court grossly erred when it read the establishment clause into the Fourteenth Amendment, thus making it applicable to the states as well as to the federal government.

Although the strict separationists may have the numerical edge today, the accommodationists have attracted a number of influential scholars and jurists. In a recent federal case, the accommodationist argument was powerful enough to convince a federal judge to disregard binding Supreme Court precedents and hold that the state of Alabama was free to support religion by requiring prayers in the public schools.[4] And although that judge's opinion was overturned by the appellate courts, Supreme Court Justice William Rehnquist has already concluded that the *Everson* "wall of separation" approach has "no historical foundation," and has called for the Court to adopt the "true meaning" of the establishment clause as shown in an accommodationist reading of its history.[5]

Though diametrically opposing each other, the strict separationists' and accommodationists' theories share a fundamental premise: That we can discern a single, clear intent behind the establishment clause. As a result, the vast majority of the debates have surrounded the search for the true intent of the First Congress of the United States in 1789. There are strong arguments on each side, and both sides discount the other's evidence as being untrue to the spirit of the establishment clause. But we must ask both sides: Is there really a single, clear intent? Instead, could the clause's political strength in the turbulent early national period be that it could have different meanings for different groups? Moreover, are the debates surrounding the remarkably noncontroversial establishment clause sufficient to give us a useful interpretive framework?

There may be elements of truth in all of the major interpretive approaches to the establishment clause, but the Supreme Court's reliance on a single intent of the Founding Fathers has forced each camp into a high-stakes battle for historical verisimilitude. As the Court's constituency changes, more justices may follow Chief Justice Rehnquist's lead; and if strict separationist history can take prayer out of the schools, accommodationist history could just as easily return it. Thus, we need to return to much travelled ground to determine whether there is a sufficiently clear intent behind the establishment clause to mandate any particular interpretation. Many of these inquiries have commenced with the late-eighteenth-century efforts in the colonies, particularly in Virginia, to separate church and state, but to begin there assumes that the establishment clause was necessarily the culmination of that process. That is, many modern interpreters have seen disestablishmentarianism as a single social movement whose intellectual force can be seen in the Enlightenment rationalism of men such as Madison and Jefferson.

Despite these attempts to root church-state relationships in a single evolutionary theory, variegated and complex factors were involved in the relationship of religion and government in the years between the first colonial settlements and the adoption of the First Amendment. Church-state conflicts began very early in the New World's settlements as dissenters of various types questioned the European pattern of state-supported churches imported by the Puritans in New England, the Dutch (and later the English) in New York, and English Anglicans throughout much of the South. Baptist Roger Williams has received much modern credit for his disputes with John Cotton on matters of church and state and, ultimately, for establishing the comparatively freethinking colony of Rhode Island. And Williams's separationist legacy, amplified a century later by fellow Baptists Isaac Backus and John Leland, has spawned an enduring school of thought holding that the "garden" of the church must be walled in for its own protection from the "wilderness" of the world. But we must not overlook the less-publicized but remarkably effective actions of the Quakers, especially in the seventeenth and eighteenth centuries. Their gathered-church tradition did not mesh well with established churches in the North or South. Showing their distaste for state-churches by means ranging from withholding taxes to running naked in the streets, the Quakers became formidable and ultimately successful disestablishmentarians in a number of the colonies.

This fascinating colonial history has been frequently expounded, most recently in Thomas John Curry's excellent *The First Freedoms: The Development of the Concepts of Freedom of Religion and Establishment of Religion in America*.[6] There is no need to retrace these footsteps except to obtain a perspective on the various social and intellectual forces at work in the more than two centuries leading up to the formal disestablishment of state churches. In reading this history, two things become apparent. First, as Curry convincingly lays out in his carefully researched book, the common church-state terminology employed in colonial and Revolutionary America had a variety of meanings. Words and phrases such as "establishment," "toleration," and "liberty of conscience" were widely used but in many different ways. North Carolinian Anglicans, for example, saw "establishment" as colony-wide tax support of the hierarchically governed Church of England. Such an establishment would have been anathema to the Congregational churches in New England, whose leaders often denied that Massachusetts's system of town-based support constituted an establishment, which they viewed as the governmental prescription of articles of faith.[7] Yet New England Baptists were no less vocal in opposition to the established "standing order" than were their Southern coreligionists. Meanwhile, "liberty of conscience" could mean anything from not hanging Quakers in Massachusetts (if they left and never came back) to the relatively tolerant society in Rhode Island. And so, we must be very careful in resurrecting the church-state insights of our colonial forebearers because they did not—as we do not—have a national consensus on the meaning of these difficult terms.

The second critical conclusion is that each church-state conflict was a local problem created by the specific circumstances of particular places. By the early nineteenth century, most of the state establishments had been severely eroded by pressure from various groups of dissenters. But the factors contributing to this erosion varied from place to place. In the South, for example, the Anglican establishment was linked in the public eye with England and was therefore seen in opposition to the popular will in the Revolutionary era. The relatively weak Anglican establishments thus suffered for political reasons only tangentially related to their ecclesiastical polity or church-state theories. Yet it was the dissenters in New England, such as the Baptists, who were portrayed by Samuel and John Adams and other patriots as subversives trying to break apart the ingrained and much stronger religious establishments in Massachusetts and Connecticut.[8]

In looking back at the long history of disestablishmentarianism, then, we must view it more as a remarkably informal coexistence of sometimes unrelated (and even conflicting) factors than as one well-organized social movement led by the Virginia gentry. Even the Virginians had their problems, as Jefferson and Madison had to battle the formidable Patrick Henry to bring down Virginia's Anglican establishment. We therefore need to search broadly to get a firm grip on the intellectual, theological, and social forces leading up to the widespread disestablishmentarian movements (plural) in late-eighteenth- and early-nineteenth-century America.

First, of course, is the European influenced Enlightenment thinking that can be seen clearly in Jefferson, Thomas Paine, and others. This intellectual rationalism—which has been given far more credit for the separation of church and state in America than it deserves—encouraged a suspicion of religion, at least to the extent of serious concern over powerful religious institutions and their clergy. For these enlightened men, the state must be protected from the clutches of the church. Religion should be allowed to rise or fall on its own, and the state must be unfettered by a church whose entanglements had historically caused intolerance and corruption. As Paine boldly put it in his *Rights of Man*: "By engendering the church with the state, a sort of mule-animal, capable only of destroying, and not of breeding up, is produced, called the *Church established by Law*. It is a stranger, even from its birth, to any parent mother, on whom it is begotten, and whom in time it kicks out and destroys." In short, church and state must be separated for the benefit of the state.[9]

The second group of disestablishmentarians—comprised primarily of Baptists and Quakers—found its theological and intellectual roots not in Enlightenment rationalism but in the gathered-church tradition of the Reformation era Anabaptists. For these colonials, the church should be a voluntary association of devout coreligionists striving to separate themselves from an evil world. Any liaison between church and state would bring the church into contact with the sin and evil inherent in the world.[10] According to Roger Williams, when there has been a "gap in the hedge or wall of separation between the garden of the church and the wilderness of the world, God hath ever broke down the wall itself, removed the candlestick, and made His garden a wilderness."[11] And so, these dissenters not only fought the establishment of other churches, but would also resist any governmental support for, or interference in, their activities.

These two schools of thought led to the same political position—disestablishment—for diametrically opposing reasons. One side sought first the preservation of the secular state, the other, the holiness of the church. Between these poles lay a third group, seeking independence of church and state for their mutual benefit. This group saw value in both churches and secular governments but had witnessed the corruption of both in European (and perhaps American) ecclesiastical establishments. James Madison spoke for the proponents of this position, arguing that the fruits of establishing Christianity have been "pride and indolence in the Clergy, ignorance and servility in the laity; in both, superstition, bigotry and persecution." And he observed that religious establishments "have been seen to erect a spiritual tyranny on the ruins of Civil authority; in many instances they have been seen upholding the thrones of political tyranny; in no instance have they been seen the guardians of the liberties of the people."[12] Although church and state could both be noble institutions, when they are combined, according to Madison, the resulting monolith is too powerful and too complacent to resist corruption and tyranny.

To these relatively well-thought-out intellectual and theological positions on church-state matters, we need to add a number of potent social forces. As historians Sidney Mead and Franklin Littell have pointed out, pragmatism and pluralism have had as much to do with church-state relations as political theory and theological doctrine.[13] For example, support for religious establishments in colonial America most often involved the payment of taxes, a national aversion since well before the Boston Tea Party. And the increasing number of dissenters, whose ranks burgeoned with the Great Awakening of the eighteenth century, brought more and more pressure to bear upon establishments often beset with internal squabbles. Intramural quarreling in the established churches not only led to public distrust and disdain but also created deep fissures within the churches themselves. It is hardly surprising that early nineteenth-century Massachusetts Trinitarian Congregationalists became less enamoured with established religion when they lost their churches in bitter disputes with the Unitarians. The separation of church and state then became almost a scorched earth policy.[14]

And we should not ignore the presence of a large number of colonials who had no particular interest in religion, or at least not in the organized churches. Whatever their ideological perspective, they would have little reason to support ecclesiastical establishments. They may not have cared enough to write tracts for scholars to ponder, but they undoubtedly contributed to the grass-roots support for those who sought—for perhaps loftier motives—to eliminate taxes for the support of churches.

All of these factors contributed to American disestablishmentarianism, and there is no way to quantify their respective contributions. But we can certainly conclude that these diverse elements were often independent aspects of the various church-state debates. The Revolution, for example, may have been a strong antiestablishment factor in Virginia but not necessarily in Massachusetts where John Adams, for one, shared Jefferson's quest for the independence of America from Britain but not of church from state. And there is no evidence that the outspoken New Englander, Isaac Backus, was even aware of Jefferson's work and its fruits in Virginia or that Madison was intimately acquainted with church-state conflicts in New England. There is no question that the late eighteenth century found many Americans opposing established churches, but we must bear in mind that they did so for many different, and often unrelated, reasons. In assessing the cultural background to the First Amendment's establishment clause, we must keep these varied perspectives in mind.

This brings us to another important factor that we tend to overlook when focusing on modern church-state problems. The "establishment" issue in seventeenth- and eighteenth-century America was the direct governmental support of a specific religious institution, most often in the form of tax revenues directed for churches.[15] A great number of establishment battles from Massachusetts to Virginia were fought over the amount of the taxes, who should be exempt from the taxes (sometimes organized dissenters such as Baptists were exempted) and who should control the distribution of the funds. Thus, disestablishment was fundamentally a shillings and pence issue and had little if anything to do with the less direct, often symbolic, links between church and state that are the subject of the Supreme Court's contemporary constitutional jurisprudence.

We must focus on two additional components of the church-state issue at the time of the Constitution's origins. One relates to the nature of the society, and the other to the nature of the government. American citizens, especially as represented by their political leaders, were a remarkably religious people in specifically Christian terms. Moreover, as numerous scholars have shown in studies on topics ranging from the Puritans to Revolutionary era preachers, the American national conscience was strongly rooted in the belief that the New World and its new nation had a divinely ordained destiny. Whether it was John Winthrop's "City on a Hill" or Ben Franklin's belief in the "Necessity of a Publick Religion," America was God's country. It was this national self-understanding that helped transform thirteen colonies into the "United States." For legislatures to invoke God's blessing or governors to proclaim days of prayer and fasting—even in specifically Protestant Christian terms—was hardly an establishment of religion for these eighteenth-century men. Rather it was simply the unself-conscious recognition of a cultural fact. That is why Benjamin Franklin, of all people, suggested that the Congress commence with a prayer and James Madison not only helped pick Congress's first chaplain but also sponsored in the Virginia legislature Thomas Jefferson's bill providing that Sabbath breakers be punished. Christianity—viewed broadly as a religion rather than any individual church—was virtually inextricably linked to American culture. And precious few attempted to say otherwise, even among the most ardent foes of established churches.[16]

And finally, we must appreciate the suspicion with which many Americans greeted the new national government. The colonies qua states were attempting to continue their union for mutual benefit, but many citizens were wary of a new political power to be superimposed over the states. Even the word "national" was touchy. The powers granted to the federal government were specifically set forth in the original Constitution, and many people clamored for amendments designed expressly to limit those powers. It was in this context of limiting the federal government in favor of the states' power that the establishment clause of the First Amendment evolved. And even then, men such as James Madison argued that no amendment was necessary because the federal government was powerless in all matters save those expressly spelled out in the Constitution. Thus, the amendments were desired and designed not fundamentally to change anything but to ensure that the status quo would be maintained.

Against this complicated landscape, we can now proceed to draw the specific figures involved in the adoption of the establishment clause, starting with the Constitutional Convention that met in Philadelphia from May to September in 1787. On August 20, Charles Pinckney of South Carolina proposed that "no religious test or qualification shall ever be annexed to any oath of office under the authority of the U.S."[17] This provision was approved, and, after review by the Committee on Style, surfaced in its final version as: "no religious Test shall ever be required as a Qualification to any Office or public Trust under the United States."[18] And that was the extent to which the Constitutional Convention dealt with the issue of religion.

The Convention's treatment of religion gave rise to several controversies, only one of which ultimately bore the fruit of a constitutional amendment. First, the Constitution was both damned and praised for its failure to mention God. The Declaration of Independence and many state constitutions gave homage to the Creator, and even a generation later the influential educator and Christian leader, Timothy Dwight, counseled the Yale senior class that it was "highly discreditable to us that we do not acknowledge God in our Constitution."[19] Constitutional amendments to rectify this snub of the Almighty have appeared periodically for the past two hundred years, often specifically calling for the recognition of Jesus Christ as Lord. None have passed.

Second, the "no religious test" provision was discussed and its scope debated. At that time, almost all of the states withheld public office—and sometimes the franchise itself—from all but Christians (a term defined differently from one place to the next and sometimes limited to Protestants).[20] The provision did not engender great controversy in the ratification process but it must certainly have been flagged as a point of distinction between how the states governed themselves and how they thought the federal government should be run. For each person who, with Major Rusk of Massachusetts, "shuddered at the idea that Roman Catholics, Papists and Pagans might be introduced into office and that Popery and the Inquisition may be established in America," there were undoubtedly others who stood with the Massachusetts Congregationalist minister, the Reverend Daniel Shute, who affirmed the belief that "there are worthy characters among men of every denomination—among the Quakers, the Baptists, the Church of England, the Papists, and even among those who have no guide, in the way to virtue and heaven, than the dictates of natural religion."[21]

We will never know exactly why the Constitutional Convention chose to adopt the "no religious test" clause, but it may be seen as a reflection of the convention's desire to avoid the mention of religion altogether or at least to make the least controversial approach to the subject. Rather than open the floor generally to those who saw religious tests as affronts to religious freedom, those who envisioned them as vital to good government, and those who could potentially debate interminably the language and scope of any proposed religious tests, the convention elected not to permit them, at least de jure. The extent to which there may be de facto religious tests even today, of course, remains an open question.

For our purposes, the most important fallout of the Constitutional Convention was its failure to address the issues of religious establishment, liberty of conscience, or any of the other individual rights many future citizens of the gestating United States wanted to be guaranteed. Although four states—Delaware, New Jersey, Georgia, and Connecticut—ratified the Constitution relatively quickly without suggesting changes, Rhode Island and North Carolina refused to ratify without the addition of a bill of rights. In other states, amendments were either officially proposed or urged by minority reports. A great deal of political history has considered the ratification process, and it is unnecessary to repeat it here. Generally speaking, there were two major camps—the Federalist supporters of the Constitution and the Antifederalist opponents. The Federalist camp counted among its number George Washington; the three famous authors of the *Federalist Papers*, Alexander Hamilton, John Jay, and James Madison; and numerous other well-known leaders. But that hardly fazed Antifederalist Patrick Henry, who announced, "The tyranny of Philadelphia [site of the Constitutional Convention] may be like the tyranny of George III."[22] Madison's portrait of the Antifederalists is no more flattering. In reporting to Thomas Jefferson on the Massachusetts ratification process, he summed up the Antifederalist attackers as composed of certain self-interested groups (such as Maine secessionists) and "partly . . . ignorant and jealous men who had been taught or had fancied, that the Convention at Philadelphia had entered into a conspiracy against the liberties of the people at large, in order to erect an aristocracy for the rich, the well born, and the men of Education."[23] Madison's portrait of the Antifederalists may be unfairly negative, but he accurately reflects both their fear of the consolidated national government and the fact that they were more an informal coalition than a well-organized political party.[24] The Antifederalists were distrustful of the new central government and therefore sought to limit its powers through a series of enumerated rights reserved to the states and the people. Liberty of conscience was but one of a number of issues on the Antifederalists' agenda; they generally wanted to make sure that the federal government kept its hands off the people and their rights, at least to the extent that those rights were guaranteed by the states. Yet although liberty of conscience was an important element of the Antifederalist litany, historian Herbert Storing has observed that "many Anti-Federalists were concerned with the maintenance of religious conviction as a support of republican government."[25] As Charles Turner wrote, "[W]ithout the prevalance of *Christian piety and morals*, the best republican Constitution can never save us from slavery and ruin."[26] In considering these opponents of the Constitution then, we must bear in mind that their distrust was directed at the new consolidated government and their commitment to religious freedom sprang not so much from opposition to churches (even established churches) but from the need for those churches to be free to inculcate morality in the American populace. Moreover, the Antifederalist impetus was not an effort to secure individual rights (a topic the state legislatures had found difficult for many decades) but to ensure that the new federal government would not interfere with the rights the states had established.[27]

Although this discussion will focus specifically on the religious establishment issue in the ratification debates, we must be very careful not to fall into the trap of assuming that the people involved in the debates cared as much about the establishment clause as we do. The discussions of religion were, by and large, few and far between, with "liberty of conscience" concerns voiced much more often than any fears of an established church. Among the volumes of newspaper articles and letters, legislative debates, pamphlets, and other written evidence of the ratification controversy, scant few pages contain even a passing reference to arguments for or against the establishment of religion.

Pennsylvania was the first state to formally consider a proposal on the subject of religion. Although Pennsylvania officially ratified the Constitution on December 12, 1787, a vocal minority constituting almost a third of the Pennsylvania convention delegates issued a dissenting report offering fourteen recommended amendments that had been rejected by the Pennsylvania convention. The first read: "The right of conscience shall be held inviolable, and neither the legislative, executive nor judicial powers of the United States shall have authority to alter, abrogate or infringe any part of the constitution of the several States, which provide for the preservation of liberty in matters of religion."[28] The proposed amendment is clearly phrased to restrict the federal government from meddling in the states' treatment of religious matters.

After the Pennsylvania convention, New Jersey, Georgia, and Connecticut ratified the Constitution without controversy over a bill of rights. Massachusetts then became the next state to reflect a sharp division between Federalists and Antifederalists on the issue of a bill of rights. The debate lasted a month and ended in a vote for ratification coupled with an official recommendation of amendments. Unlike the Philadelphia minority proposals, the Massachusetts amendments were drafted by the Federalists as a compromise in the effort to win enough votes for ratification. The amendments were written by Federalist Theophilus Parsons and introduced by John Hancock, who leaned towards the Antifederalist position. Historical evidence is unclear as to whether the Massachusetts proposals were influenced by the Pennsylvanian minority report.[29] In any event, they were hardly as far reaching as the Pennsylvania minority's proposals. The right to liberty of conscience, for example, was not mentioned, although it had been included in an amendment offered by Samuel Adams and defeated by the convention. The final vote was close (187 to 168) in favor of ratification with the recommendation that Hancock's amendments be added to "remove the fears and quiet the apprehensions of many of the good people of the commonwealth, and more effectually to guard against an undue administration of the federal government."[30]

Of particular note in the Massachusetts ratification process was the presence of avid church-state spokesman and ardent disestablishmentarian Isaac Backus. In his one foray into elective office, the Reverend Mr. Backus represented the town of Middleborough in the convention. Elected as an Antifederalist, Backus was converted at the convention to support the Constitution.[31] In later explaining to his constituents his failure to insist on an antiestablishment clause, Backus drew on a very broad reading of the "no religious test" provision. As historian William McLoughlin notes, "The constitution [Backus] explained, guaranteed freedom and stability while it prohibited any religious establishment: 'no such way of worship can be established without any religious test.' "[32] Needless to say, Backus's broad reading of the "no religious test" clause has not enjoyed a large following through constitutional history.

Maryland became the seventh state to ratify the Constitution on April 26, 1788, and its large Federalist majority shouted down a proposal to add amendments to the ratification. Although a committee was subsequently formed to consider amendments, none were approved. The committee's thirteen proposals, together with fifteen additions urged by the minority, were published privately as a pamphlet and were widely distributed. Among the fifteen minority additions which had been voted down by the committee as a whole was a proposal "That there be no national religion established by law; but that all persons be equally entitled to protection in their religious liberty."[33]

South Carolina ratified the Constitution a month after Maryland with four recommended amendments, one of which dealt with religion: "Resolved that the third section of the Sixth Article ought to be amended by inserting the word "other" between the words 'no' and 'religious.' "[34] The intended breadth of this amendment is unclear. On its face, it refers back to Article VI's mandate that officers of the government "shall be bound by Oath or Affirmation, to support this Constitution." So as not to denigrate the religious nature of the "Oath or Affirmation" the South Carolinians may have wanted to insert the word "other" for clarification. In other words, there would be no religious test for office other than the requirement of an "Oath or Affirmation." Roger Sherman of Connecticut lauded this emendation as ingenious, and suggested that "it may be considered as a clerical omission and be inserted without calling a convention; as it stands the effect will be the same."[35] Sherman's de minimus amendment procedure did not catch on, and others have read the amendment as having a much broader sweep. Antieau, Downey, and Roberts in *Freedom From Federal Establishment*, for example, argue that the simple amendment was intended to convey a position that would forbid preferential, but not nondenominational, support for religion. They note that the proposal was introduced by the Reverend Mr. Francis Cummins, a Presbyterian minister, who said,

> Would it not have assumed all the intended purposes of the expanded hearts of the convention as to civil and religious freedom to have said "but no religious denominations shall ever have preference to another in matters of state, and all religious societies shall have equal liberty and protection." This . . . would be an everlasting security against persecution and dissention upon religious accounts, and at the same time in no degree literally or otherwise, break in upon . . . the sacred

nature of an oath even at civil bar. . . . Mr. President. One single word of amendment would perfectly satisfy me here.[36]

It seems unlikely that all of the Reverend Mr. Cummins's colleagues believed that they were enacting his nonestablishment views in adopting the one-word amendment, but this episode shows the seriousness with which at least some modern commentators have sought to endow each word of the Founding Fathers with several paragraphs of meaning.

New Hampshire, which ratified the Constitution on June 21, 1788, became the ninth state to do so, thus officially making the document effective. The record of New Hampshire's proceedings is unfortunately sparse, but it does show a series of recommended amendments. Of the twelve proposals, the first nine were virtually the same as those offered by Massachusetts. One of the three new amendments dealt with the subject of religion in a way suggestive of the ultimate First Amendment language: "Congress shall make no Laws touching Religion or to infringe the rights of Conscience."[37] We have no clue, however, as to the debates surrounding this proposal or even as to its author, although Samuel Livermore, a leading Federalist at the New Hampshire convention, later introduced this language in the First Congress in place of James Madison's proposals.

Although New Hampshire's vote had formal significance in effecting the union, the inclusion of the Commonwealth of Virginia was a practical necessity for the success of the new nation, and ratification was hardly assured. Patrick Henry led the Antifederalist charge, insisting in speeches up to seven hours long that the national government would trample on the rights of the people. As usual, liberty of conscience was identified among the primary lacunae of the Constitution. The Federalists argued that the national government was limited to its enumerated powers—none of which gave authority over religious matters—and that a bill of rights would be scant protection against any government bent on tyranny. Echoing his position in *Federalist* 10, Madison, for example, pointed to "the multiplicity of sects" as "the best and only security for religious liberty in any society."[38] Then, noting that he believed a majority of citizens of Virginia and the other states to be "decidedly against any exclusive establishment," he concluded,

It is better that [religious freedom] should be depended upon from the general legislature, than from one particular state. *A particular state might concur in one religious project.* But the United States abound in such a variety of sects, that it is a strong security against religious persecution; and it is sufficient to authorize a conclusion, that no one sect will ever be able to outnumber or depress the rest.[39] (emphasis added)

Accommodationists can rally around the "exclusive establishment" language and the suggestion that a state, as opposed to the federal government, might "concur in a religious project."

Ultimately, Virginia ratified the Constitution on June 25, 1788, without requiring amendments, although "to relieve the apprehensions of those who may be solicitous for amendment," a committee was appointed to make recommendations. The committee numbered twenty men, including such notables as George Wythe, Patrick Henry, George Mason, James Madison, John Marshall, and James Monroe. Two days later (suggesting more than a little advanced planning), the committee reported back with a comprehensive plan for improving the Constitution. In addition to twenty specific amendments to the original document, the committee proposed a bill of rights "asserting, and securing from encroachment, the essential rights of the people." The last of the twenty items of the bill of rights reads:

> That religion, or the duty which we owe to our Creator, and the manner of discharging it, can be directed only by reason and conviction, not by force or violence; and therefore all men have an equal, natural and unalienable right to the free exercise of religion, according to the dictates of conscience, *and that no particular religious sect or society ought to be favored or established, by law, in preference to others*.[40] (emphasis added)

This, of course, closely parallels Article 16 of the Virginia Declaration of Rights adopted twelve years earlier.[41] In fact, the two are virtually identical down to the last phrase; but since Virginia's religious establishment endured for a decade past the Declaration of Rights, the final language in the declaration read: "and that it is the mutual duty of all to practice Christian forebearance, love, and charity, towards each other."[42] When the Virginians turned their eye towards the federal government, and after the disestablishmentarians had triumphed in the commonwealth, the issue of establishment was apparently more important than "Christian forebearance." While this change certainly put another arrow in the federal nonestablishment quiver, accommodationists can point to Virginia's "no particular religious sect or society" language as evidence of the Founding Fathers' intent only to forbid preferential establishments, thus leaving the government free to provide nondenominational support to religion.[43]

New York was the next state to ratify the Constitution, but not without controversy. Despite the presence of noted Federalist spokesmen such as John Jay and Alexander Hamilton, Antifederalist sentiment was extremely strong. To ward off the possibility that ratification would either be defeated or made conditional on certain amendments, the Federalists agreed to attach a bill of rights to the ratification resolution as well as a lengthy list of amendments. Included in the bill of rights drafted by Antifederalist John

Lansing was the following on the subject of religion: "That the People have an equal, natural and unalienable right, freely and peaceably to Exercise their Religion according to the dictates of Conscience, and that no Religious Sect or Society ought to be favoured or established by Law in preference of others."[44] The similarity to Virginia's provision is readily apparent.

Finally, North Carolina decided to withhold formal judgment on the Constitution. The Antifederalists so dominated the North Carolina convention that unconditional ratification was a virtual impossibility. Instead, the North Carolinians approved a long list of amendments and a bill of rights taken verbatim, for the most part, from Virginia's proposals, and then pronounced that "this Convention has thought proper neither to ratify nor reject the Constitution."[45]

It is with this complicated background that the First Congress met in 1789 to carry on the affairs of the new government, and the adoption of amendments to the Constitution was an important agenda item. Antifederalists were a potent political force in many of the states, and for the stability of the union, they needed to be placated and comforted by amendments designed to show the limited power of the national government. Since the Federalist opposition to amendments had been based primarily on the self-evident nature of the limitedness of federal power and not on an aversion to individual liberties generally, the likelihood of a bill of rights passing the First Congress was extremely high.

Scholar Bernard Schwartz has catalogued 210 separate amendments recommended either officially or unofficially by the states, covering almost one hundred substantive items.[46] Six of the states had dealt with the subject of religion, but only four formally included establishment clauses and one, Maryland, specifically rejected such a provision. Virginia and North Carolina submitted identical proposals ("no particular religious sect or society ought to be favored or established, by law, in preference to others"); New York's proposal was very similar ("no Religious Sect or Society ought to be favoured or established by Law in preference of others"); New Hampshire suggested something considerably different ("Congress shall make no Laws touching Religion"); and Maryland considered but did not approve a nonestablishment amendment ("there [shall] be no national religion established by law").[47]

Precious little legislative history has been preserved (perhaps it never existed) to help us interpret these proposals that were, without question, sine qua non with respect to the First Amendment's establishment clause. At least four of the thirteen states desired to some extent to forbid a national religious establishment. Yet only one, New Hampshire, wanted the government's hands completely off religion (no "touching"). Other states bothering to propose nonestablishment clauses referred only to the establishment of one religion to the exclusion of others.

But we should be wary of any simplistic reading of these proposals. The ratification controversy was a broad one over the nature and power of the new national government. While liberty of conscience was a commonly acknowledged right of the people (however it was defined from place to place), the issue of establishment simply was not at the forefront of any ratification debate. Practically speaking, the most likely reason for this lack of attention is that few people, if any, saw any reasonable threat of a *national* religious establishment. As a result, once any amendments were offered, the inclusion or exclusion of an establishment clause was of relatively little consequence. Either because of the diversity of religious sentiments, as Madison posited, or on account of any number of intellectual, political, or religious motives, there was no national religious establishment—or even a national establishment *issue*. Yet, as a number of states would continue to demonstrate over the succeeding two score years, efforts to eliminate state religious establishments created very lively and often acrimonious controversy. Any proposed federal establishment would be easily defeated and was thus a powerless nonentity; on the other hand, the state-supported churches had well-entrenched economic and political vested interests. The real disestablishment battle would be fought another day. At the Constitutional Conventions, the states merely sought to instruct the national government on how individual liberties must be preserved.

Although the mandate for a national nonestablishment clause was minimal at best, we should nevertheless review the First Congress's proceedings on the subject since they have assumed such great importance in the eyes of modern commentators. In doing so, however, we must keep the nature of the historical record in perspective. All we have is the *Annals of Congress*, a compilation of newspaper reports that relied on less than precise eighteenth-century shorthand and were undoubtedly subject to paraphrase at best and blatant errors at worst. Historian Leonard Levy quotes Madison on the "mutilation & perversion" of the newspaper accounts of the congressional debates. We will probably never know how accurate these sources are, but they are all we have.[48]

As every history book on this subject points out, Virginia's James Madison took responsibility for preparing a bill of rights for submission to the First Congress. On June 8, 1789, after a lengthy prolegomenon on the popular support for amendments to the Constitution, Representative James Madison introduced a series of proposals. The fourth item was a suggestion that between the third and fourth clauses of the ninth section of the first article the following should be added: "The civil rights of none shall be abridged on account of religious belief or worship, nor shall any national religion be established, nor shall the full and equal rights of conscience be in any manner, or on any pretext, infringed."[49] Then, after providing for the right of peaceable assembly, the right to bear arms, and a number of other elements of what has become the first ten amendments to the Constitution, his fifth proposal stated "No State shall violate the equal rights of conscience."[50]

We do not know how Madison came up with his proposals on the subject of religion. While several of the states had either recommended or considered establishment clauses, only Maryland's defeated proposal had used the "national religion" language adopted by Madison. Nor had any of the states suggested that the federal government should have authority to regulate the state's treatment of liberty of conscience.

According to the *Annals of Congress*, over two months passed before the Congress took up debate on Madison's religion proposals. Then, on Saturday, August 15, the legislators considered an amendment reading, "[N]o religion shall be established by law, nor shall the equal rights of conscience be infringed."[51] The record discloses no explanation as to why the word *national* disappeared, and the reports of the debate suggest that the Congressmen may have devoted only desultory attention to the entire establishment matter. There appear to be no well-defined battle lines or serious points of contention. The recorded debate hardly contains the lofty or acrimonious rhetoric associated either with efforts to disestablish state churches at that time or with modern church-state discussions. Rather, the Founding Fathers seemed to focus on relatively simple linguistic points and issues tangential to what we might see as the critical issues in the relationship of church and state. The reason is undoubtedly that a prohibition of a national religious establishment was a nonissue because no one favored the concept. In a list of amendments seen as unnecessary and redundant by the Federalists, a nonestablishment clause would certainly have been near the top.

Sylvester was the first to respond to Madison's proposal, and his concerns were semantic. Expressing doubts as to the "mode of expression," he was worried that, contrary to the amendment's intent, "it might be thought to have a tendency to abolish religion altogether." Vining then suggested that the two clauses be transposed so the equal rights of conscience would have top billing. And Gerry wanted the clause to read "no religious doctrine shall be established by law."[52]

To this point, the record shows only these essentially unrelated comments, none of which generated any response or debate. Then Sherman, a staunch Connecticut Federalist, awakened a little interest by arguing that the amendment was "altogether unnecessary, inasmuch as Congress had no authority whatever delegated to them by the constitution to make religious establishments," and he moved to have it stricken. This, of course, was the classic Federalist position.[53] Carroll took up the cudgel, asserting that "the rights of conscience are, in their nature, of peculiar delicacy, and will little bear the gentlest touch of governmental hand." Moreover, Carroll noted that "many sects have concurred in opinion that they are not well secured under the present constitution," and therefore, he would support the substance of the amendment although he was not particular about the language. Carroll observed that this amendment "would tend more towards conciliating the minds of the people to the Government than almost any other amendment he had heard proposed." At least as to the establishment clause, Carroll's statement is difficult to reconcile with the states' ratification debates, but he may have been speaking primarily about liberty of conscience, a more central concern in the state proceedings.[54]

James Madison stepped in to address the federalism issue, observing that "[w]hether the words are necessary or not, he did not mean to say, but they had been required by some of the State Conventions, who seemed [to believe that the Constitution's "necessary and proper" clause enabled Congress] to make laws of such a nature as might infringe the rights of conscience, and establish a national religion." In Madison's opinion, the amendment meant that "Congress should not establish religion, and enforce the legal observation of it by law, nor compel men to worship God in any manner contrary to their conscience."[55]

Huntington, harking back to Sylvester's initial comment, feared that the amendment would be misconstrued to the detriment of churches relying on members' contributions. A court might consider the enforcement of a church member's pledge to be a religious establishment. But freedom from establishment, he continued, had a salutary effect on Rhode Island, and Huntington hoped for such an amendment "to secure the rights of conscience, and a free exercise of the rights of religion, but not to patronize those who professed no religion at all."[56]

To pacify those who feared harm to organized religion, Madison recommended a return to his original form of amendment by inserting "national" before "religion." In explanation, he noted his belief that "the people feared one sect might obtain a pre-eminence, or two combine together, and establish a religion to which they would compel others to conform." By adding the word "national," it would "point the amendment directly to the object it was intended to prevent."[57]

Samuel Livermore of New Hampshire, wishing not "to dwell long on the subject," offered his state's proposed religion amendment (with a minor linguistic change) in place of Madison's. It read, "Congress shall make no laws touching religion, or infringing the rights of conscience."[58]

Gerry and Madison had a short dispute over the meaning and use of the word "national," since it had achieved some notoriety in the Federalist-Antifederalist debates, and Madison withdrew his suggestion of adding that controversial term. And, then, without further recorded debate, the House of Representatives, sitting as a Committee of the Whole, passed Livermore's proposal by a vote of thirty-one to twenty. Of the fifty-one members voting, only eight appear to have entered the debate.[59]

Two days later, on Monday, August 17, 1789, the Congress considered

Madison's proposal that "no State shall infringe the equal rights of conscience." Tucker strongly objected on the grounds that it would be better "to leave the State Governments to themselves, and not to interfere with them any more than we already do." Madison defended the proposal as "the most valuable amendment in the whole list. If there was any reason to restrain the Government of the United States from infringing on these essential rights, it was equally necessary that they should be secured against the State Governments." Finally, Livermore recommended that the clause be reversed to read "the equal rights of conscience . . . shall not be infringed by any State." This revision met with general agreement and was adopted without further debate.[60]

Later that week, without any recorded debate, the "fourth amendment" (i.e., the establishment and free exercise clauses) was adopted in a revised version proffered by Ames of Massachusetts: "Congress shall make no law establishing religion, or to prevent the free exercise thereof, or to infringe the rights of conscience."[61]

This was the extent of the debate concerning the establishment clause as it was offered for the Senate's consideration. Two antiestablishment clauses had been approved by the House, both introduced by New Englanders—Samuel Livermore of New Hampshire and Fisher Ames of Massachusetts. While these men showed no support for a national religious establishment, their states had well-entrenched religious establishments that would endure for some decades after the adoption of the Bill of Rights. Why they were so interested in an amendment preventing Congress from establishing a religion, or even "touching" religion in Livermore's case, is unknown.

A couple of weeks later, the *Senate Journal* provided sparse reporting of the Senate's consideration of the House's proposals. Although the *Journal* does not expressly state the language of the amendment being considered, it probably read as follows: "Congress shall make no law establishing religion or prohibiting the free exercise thereof, nor shall the rights of conscience be infringed." This, of course, bore close resemblance to the Ames proposal, after some minor adjustments.[62]

After two attempts, the Senate changed the first part of the clause to resemble the amendments recommended after ratification by Virginia, North Carolina, and New York. The new version then became, "Congress shall make no law establishing one religious sect or society in preference to others, nor shall the rights of conscience be infringed." There followed a motion to strike the amendment in its entirety, but the motion failed. Another motion proposed a transposition of the "establishment" and "conscience" clauses, and it also failed, as did one to read as follows: "Congress shall make no law establishing any particular denomination of religion in preference to another, or prohibiting the free exercise thereof, nor shall the rights of conscience be infringed." Finally, the equal rights of conscience clause was eliminated. With that action, the debate ended for the day.[63]

Several days later, the Senate rejected, without any record of debate, the House's proposal of prohibiting the states from infringing the rights of conscience.[64]

Then, on September 9, 1789, again without any record of the debate, the Senate voted to amend the religion clauses as follows: "Congress shall make no law establishing articles of faith or a mode of worship, or prohibiting the free exercise of religion."[65] Modern commentators have pointed to this new version as the triumph of a faction in the Senate who wanted to allow the government to provide nondenominational financial support to religion.[66] Again, there is no available evidence to back up such speculation. In any event, this left the House and Senate with different versions, and a conference committee was appointed to work out this and other amendments. The committee, whose deliberations were not recorded, numbered six people, three from each chamber. Charles Carroll (Maryland), Oliver Ellsworth (Connecticut), and William Paterson (New Jersey) represented the Senate, and James Madison (Virginia), Roger Sherman (Connecticut), and John Vining (Delaware) represented the House. Within a week, the House and Senate had agreed to amend the Constitution to include the following, which is the current form of the religion clauses of the First Amendment: "Congress shall make no law respecting an establishment of religion, or prohibiting the free exercise thereof."[67] There is some evidence that the House held out for this language in lieu of the Senate's proposal, but we have no supporting rationale. And since we have no useful record of the state ratification debates over the Bill of Rights, that concludes the uninspiring legislative history of the establishment clause.[68]

What can we conclude from this analysis of the Founding Fathers' views of the First Amendment's establishment clause? Mainly that modern commentators have made a Constitutional mountain out of a congressional molehill. We do not even have enough evidence to conclude whether the clause was viewed by its framers as fundamentally opposed to establishments of religion or supportive of state religious establishments seeking to avoid federal regulation. On one hand, we could argue for an intent to ensure that the federal government would not give the same kind of favored treatment to religion (generally Protestant Christianity in one form or another) that a number of the states were then providing or had recently provided. And the reason so to restrict the federal government might not have been philosophical aversion to the concept of a state-supported church but rather fear that a national government would favor the *wrong* church. On the other hand, we could trace the "respecting" an establishment language back to Livermore's "touching" and posit that this crafty New Englander had the clause worded specifically to protect state establishments from federal interference.

Scholar Michael Malbin argues this as cogently as anyone, and his position is supported to some extent by Anson Phelps Stokes, author of an important three-volume treatise on church-state relations in America, who asserts that Livermore has "received almost no public credit for his services in suggesting the essential part of the phraseology of our religious freedom guarantee."[69] These writers owe the initial insight (if not to Livermore himself) to nineteenth-century Supreme Court Justice Joseph Story, who wrote in his influential *Commentaries on the Constitution* that "the whole power over the subject of religion is left exclusively to the state governments, to be acted upon according to their own sense of justice, and the state constitutions.[70] Malbin also argues that the Founding Fathers conveyed a critical message by prohibiting "an" establishment as opposed to "the" establishment of religion. He argues, "Had the framers prohibited 'the establishment of religion,' which would have emphasized the generic word 'religion,' there might have been some reason for thinking they wanted to prohibit all official preferences of religion over irreligion."[71] Since they did not, Malbin continues, "they were showing that they wanted to prohibit only those official activities that tended to promote the interests of one or another particular sect."[72] While Malbin's argument is imaginative, I find it unconvincing.

In fact, all of these suggestions about how to interpret the establishment clause based on the framers' intentions are just short of complete speculation because they are based solely on the extremely sparse and highly questionable historical records. The records simply contain too little evidence. To the extent that we can broadly read the sense of the secondhand historical documents, they most clearly show a lack of interest amounting virtually to apathy towards the establishment clause. Both Levy and Curry agree as to the "inattentiveness and absentmindness" (Curry's words) with which Americans handled the religion clauses of the First Amendment. But this does not stop Levy from clearly identifying a legislative intent or Curry from suggesting at least a general understanding of the "establishment" terminology at the time of the adoption of the First Amendment. And for Curry, "the meaning of the First Amendment must arise out of its historical context rather than from a literalist reading."[73] In his opinion, "[T]he people of almost every state that ratified the First Amendment believed that religion should be maintained and supported voluntarily. They saw government attempts to organize and regulate such support as a usurpation of power and a violation of liberty of conscience and free exercise of religion, and as falling within the scope of what they termed an establishment of religion."[74]

Most commentators have found clear messages in the words of the Founding Fathers and usually excoriate those who see things differently.

Robert L. Cord, for example, describes the prominent work of church-state lawyer and avid separationist Leo Pfeffer as "overbroad" and "invalid," and calls Justice Black's *Everson* opinion "fiction."[75] Leonard Levy then takes up the hot iron and brands Cord's work, in a play on the title, "historical fiction masquerading as scholarship."[76] This is a high-stakes battle, and few bother to mince words.

Generally speaking, I find Curry to be the most persuasive of the commentators, but I am unwilling to infuse the establishment clause with as much late-eighteenth-century meaning as he does. It is just as wrong to assume that the establishment clause meant (or now means) what Americans generally thought the word "establishment" meant at the time the clause was adopted as it is to read the church-state philosophy of James Madison or Samuel Livermore directly into the First Amendment. We must not forget that even fervent disestablishmentarian James Madison seemed content with almost any form of amendment, since he had thought it unnecessary in the first place. The language of all of the proposals in the First Congress was vague and susceptible to many interpretations. And no one seemed to care.

Had the Founding Fathers possessed the foresight to predict the multitude of interpretations we have tried to read back into their minds, they might have given us carefully crafted dissertations covering everything from the nascent public school movement to public Christmas displays. Or they might never have reached any consensus (or even majority vote) on the form of an establishment clause if they had been forced to agree on what it really meant. The Founding Fathers simply did not think they were doing anything particularly noteworthy. In modern argot, it was no big deal. There was no national disestablishmentarian movement or cohesive impetus for a nonestablishment clause. And we err the most when we assume that there was. No matter what the Supreme Court and modern commentators have found in the way of "proof texts," there is no clear mandate and hardly any useful guidance to be found in the records of the adoption of the establishment clause. Unfortunately, judges, lawyers, scholars, and many others continue to try to cram volumes of meaning into ten words virtually devoid of clear intent on the historical record before us. This, of course, does not eliminate the need to interpret and apply this vital part of the Constitution. But we must cure ourselves of the desire to invoke the Founding Fathers as the last word on interpretation. That august group gave us merely the first few words, and remarkably few of them at that.

NOTES

1. Everson v. Board of Education, 330 U.S. 1 (1947), reh. denied, 330 U.S. 855 (1947). The strict separationists' most influential and prolific advocate is probably constitutional lawyer Leo Pfeffer. See, for example, Leo Pfeffer, *Church, State*

and Freedom, rev. ed. (Boston: Beacon Press, 1967). Pfeffer has acted as counsel for numerous parties in church-state litigation at the Supreme Court level. Leonard Levy, whose work is discussed later at greater length, has written the most recent work of strict separationist scholarship. Leonard Levy, *The Establishment Clause: Religion and the First Amendment* (New York: Macmillan, 1986).

Commentators on the establishment clause are legion, and it would be virtually impossible to refer to all of them. Throughout the text and notes, I have tried to cite a number of the works that have proved influential, but neither this chapter nor the bibliography is by any means inclusive. I have tried, however, to bring up most of the noteworthy arguments in the debate, all of which focus on the same historical evidence.

2. Madison's "Memorial and Remonstrance" was written in 1784 in response to a proposal of the Virginia legislature to levy a tax to support "Teachers of the Christian Religion." The bill was proposed by Patrick Henry and had the support of many leading Virginians, including George Washington, John Marshall, and Richard Henry Lee. The "Memorial and Remonstrance" was circulated as a petition and did not bear Madison's name as author. The precise amount of its influence is debatable (it appears to have generated 1552 signatures, while another petition bore 4899), but Madison certainly was an influential opponent of church-state ties. Ultimately, not only was the bill voted down, but the surge of antiestablishment thought caused enactment of Jefferson's Act for Establishing Religious Freedom, which had lain dormant since 1779. See William T. Hutchinson et al., *The Papers of James Madison*, 13 vols. (Chicago: University of Chicago Press, 1962–69), vol. 8, pp. 195, 297, 401 (ed. notes); Pfeffer, *Church, State and Freedom*, p. 113; Marvin K. Singleton, "Colonial Virginia as First Amendment Matrix: Henry, Madison and Assessment Establishment," and Donald L. Drakeman, "Religion and the Republic: James Madison and the First Amendment," both originally appearing in the *Journal of Church and State* and reprinted in Robert S. Alley, ed., *James Madison on Religious Liberty* (Buffalo, N.Y.: Prometheus Books, 1985), pp. 157–172, 231–247. The preamble of the Bill for Establishing Religious Freedom emphasizes "that the opinions of men are not the subject of civil government," and the text itself reads: "that no man shall be compelled to frequent or support any religious worship, place or ministry whatsoever, nor shall be enforced, restrained, molested, or burthened in his body or goods, nor shall otherwise suffer, on account of his religious opinions or belief; but that all men shall be free to profess, and by argument to maintain, their opinions in matters of religion, and that the same shall in no wise diminish, enlarge or affect their civil capacities." Julian P. Boyd, ed., *The Papers of Thomas Jefferson* (Princeton, N.J.: Princeton University Press, 1950), vol. 2, 1777 to June 18, 1779.

3. Robert L. Cord, *Separation of Church and State: Historical Fact and Current Fiction* (New York: Lambeth Press, 1982), p. 50. Cord's work represents one of the more recent accommodationist efforts, and it has been cited by federal judges and portions have been read into the *Congressional Record*. As on the strict separationist side, there are many accommodationist books and articles, including Chester James Antieau, Arthur T. Downey, and Edward C. Roberts, *Freedom from Federal Establishment: Formation and Early History of the First Amendment Religion Clauses* (Milwaukee, 1964); Walter F. Berns, *The First Amendment and the Future of American Democracy* (New York: Basic Books, 1976); and Rodney

Smith, *Public Prayer and the Constitution: A Case Study in Constitutional Interpretation* (Wilmington Del.: Scholarly Resources, 1987).

4. Jaffree v. James, 554 F. Supp. 1104 (S.D. Ala. 1983), rev'd Jaffree v. Wallace, 705 F.2d 1156 (11th Cir. 1983), aff'd Wallace v. Jaffree, 466 U.S. 924 (1984) and 86 L.Ed. 2d 29 (1985). Judge Brevard Hand's opinion stated that "the Court agrees with the studied conclusions of Dr. Cord that 'it should be clear that the traditional interpretation of Madison and Jefferson is historically faulty if not virtually unfounded.' " 554 F. Supp. at 1117.

5. Wallace v. Jaffree, 86 L.Ed. 2d 29, 66–80. Justice Rehnquist concluded, "The Framers intended the Establishment Clause to prohibit the designation of any church as a 'national' one. The Clause was also designed to stop the Federal Government from asserting a preference for one religious denomination or sect over others. . . . [N]othing in the Establishment Clause requires government to be strictly neutral between religion and irreligion, nor does that Clause prohibit Congress or the States from pursuing legitimate secular ends through nondiscriminatory sectarian means." 86 L.Ed. 2d 29, p. 80. Accordingly, states should be permitted to regulate the public schools by prescribing a classroom prayer.

6. Thomas John Curry, *The First Freedoms: The Development of the Concepts of Freedom of Religion and Establishment of Religion in America* (New York: Oxford University Press, 1986).

7. See Curry, *First Freedoms*, p. 209 et seq. Nevertheless, Curry concludes that "America both before and after the Revolution thought of establishment as an exclusive preference for one religion" (p. 209). He thus criticizes modern scholars who have read back into the minds of the framers a debate over "exclusive establishments" (government support for a particular denomination) versus "nonpreferential establishments" (those awarding governmental support to religion generally). Curry's dissertation advisor, Leonard Levy, while calling Curry's work the "best book on the subject," disagrees that the exclusive establishment language was preeminent at the time of the framing of the First Amendment. Rather, according to Levy, "An establishment of religion meant to those who framed and ratified the First Amendment what it meant in [the seven states in the Union as of 1791 that maintained establishments], and in all seven it meant public support of religion on a non preferential basis. It was specifically this public support on a non preferential basis that the establishment clause of the First Amendment sought to forbid." Levy, *Establishment*, p. xvi. See also Leonard W. Levy, *Judgments: Essays on American Constitutional History* (Chicago: Quadrangle Books, 1972), a collection of essays including ones on "No Establishment of Religion: The Original Understanding" and "School Prayers and the Founding Fathers."

8. According to church historian Franklin Littell, "When Isaac Backus presented the cause of the Baptists before the Continental Congress in Philadelphia in 1774, John Adams commented 'that one might as well expect a change in the solar system as that the great Puritan Commonwealth would abolish its ecclesiastical laws,' and Samuel Adams inferred that the complaints came from enthusiasts who made it a merit to suffer persecution." Franklin H. Littell, *From State Church to Pluralism* (New York: Doubleday, 1962), pp. 36–37, citing Henry S. Burrage, "The Contest for Religious Liberty in Massachusetts," *Papers of the American Society of Church History* 6 (1893), p. 156.

9. Paine is quoted in Anson Phelps Stokes, *Church and State in the United*

States (New York: Harper & Bros., 1950), vol. 1, p. 321. This multiple school of thought approach to the religion clauses is not new, either for historians or lawyers. See, for example, Robert T. Handy, "The Magna Charta of Religious Freedom in America," *Union Seminary Quarterly Review* 38 (1984), pp. 301–17; and Laurence Tribe, *American Constitutional Law* (Long Island, N.Y.: Foundation Press, 1978).

10. This is probably best categorized in H. Richard Niebuhr's phrase, "Christ Against Culture." See H. Richard Niebuhr, *Christ and Culture* (New York: Harper & Bros., 1951), pp. 45–82. Niebuhr traces this position back to the First Letter of John, Tertullian, and others who focus strongly on the contradiction between the world and the Word of God. Separation of church and state is then a necessary subset of the fundamental need to separate the faithful from the world.

11. Quoted in Mark DeWolfe Howe, *The Garden and the Wilderness: Religion and Government in Constitutional History* (Chicago: University of Chicago Press, 1965), p. 5.

12. Hutchinson et al., eds., *The Papers of James Madison*, 13 vols. (Chicago: University of Chicago Press, 1962–69), vol. 8, pp. 299–300.

13. See, for example, Sidney E. Mead, *The Lively Experiment: The Shaping of Christianity in America* (New York: Harper & Row, 1963). Littell not only emphasizes pluralism but he focuses special attention on revivalism as a central factor in breaking up European patterns of church-state relations. He writes, "[T]he churches accustomed themselves but slowly and reluctantly to the prospect of voluntary support of religious education and church life. Again and again, confronted by special problems or opportunities, they reverted to the old custom of using government or tax monies to support church work. It was the revivals, however, that made voluntaryism a possibility. They brought the laity alive and produced a sympathetic co-operation of clergy and laity such as the best of the establishment rarely saw." Littell, *From State Church to Pluralism*, p. 55.

14. Littell points out that the famous *Dedham* case in Massachusetts (1819–20), in which "the Trinitarian Congregationalists lost to the Unitarian Congregationalists all but a handful of church properties within fifty miles of Boston," led to a "willingness on the part of Massachusetts Christendom to abandon state-church ways. The last appropriation of tax monies to support Christian (Unitarian) and theological education at Harvard was made in 1834." Littell, *From State Church to Pluralism*, p. 8.

15. See Levy, *Judgments*, p. 202. ("An establishment of religion in America at the time of the framing of the Bill of Rights meant government aid and sponsorship of religion, principally by impartial tax support of the institutions of religion, the churches.")

16. This link between religion and the republic has received considerable attention over the past decade. See, for example, Robert Bellah, "Civil Religion in America," *Daedalus* 96 (Winter 1967) pp. 1–21; and John F. Wilson, *Public Religion in American Culture* (Philadelphia: Temple University Press, 1984). William Lee Miller counters that "the late eighteenth century was a low point, a kind of religious depression, in American religious history, with sparse church membership and attendance." William Lee Miller, *The First Liberty: Religion and the American Republic* (New York: Knopf, 1986), p. 127. It is unclear how closely related religious belief and church membership are, but the strength of the links between

religion and the republic surviving even to this day suggests that our "City on a Hill" roots are deep indeed. For more on this subject, see chapter 4 and, for example, Sacvan Bercovitch, *The American Jeremiad* (Madison, Wis.: University of Wisconsin Press, 1978); Nathan O. Hatch, *The Sacred Cause of Liberty: Republican Thought and the Millennium in Revolutionary New England* (New Haven, Conn.: Yale University Press, 1977); Robert N. Bellah, *The Broken Covenant: American Civil Religion in Time of Trial* (New York: Seabury Press, 1975).

17. Jonathon Elliot, ed., *The Debates in the Several State Conventions on the Adoption of the Federal Constitution*, 5 vols. (Washington, D.C., 1836), vol. 5, p. 456. In addition, Madison's notes and Elliot's *Debates* record a plan for the Constitution offered by Charles Pinckney on May 23, 1787, that included several rights later embodied in the first ten amendments. Among other things, he is recorded as proposing that "[t]he legislature of the United States shall pass no law on the subject of religion" Elliot, *Debates*, vol. 5, p. 131. Citing Charles Warren, *The Making of the Constitution* (Boston: Little, Brown, 1928), Leonard Levy concludes that the Pinckney plan was "spurious." Levy, *Establishment*, p. 202 (note 1); Levy, *Judgments*, p. 218 (note 7). Since we have no background or debates, spurious or otherwise, the Pinckney proposal is probably irrelevant to our inquiry, whether or not it was actually introduced at the Constitutional Convention.

18. U.S. Const. Art. VI; Farrard, II, 579. Madison's notes show that North Carolina voted against this provision and that Maryland was divided. Hunt, and Scott, ed., *Madison's Notes on the Debates in the Federal Convention* (New York, 1920), p. 495.

19. President Dwight's Decisions of Questions discussed by the senior class in Yale College in 1813 and 1814, p. iii quoted in Anson Phelps Stokes, *Church and State in the United States*, 3 vols. (New York: Harper & Bros., 1950), vol. 1, p. 523.

20. For a discussion of a number of these provisions around the time of the Convention, see Antieau, Downey, and Roberts, *Freedom*, pp. 92–98.

21. Quoted in Antieau, Downey, and Roberts, *Freedom*, pp. 100–101.

22. Elliot, *Debates*, vol. 3, p. 436.

23. Quoted in Bernard Schwartz, *The Bill of Rights: A Documentary History* (New York: Chelsea House, 1971), vol. 2, p. 725.

24. Historian Gordon Wood has noted that the very existence of a substantial body of Antifederalists is surprising. "[I]n the face of the preponderance of wealth and respectability in support of the Constitution, what remains extraordinary about 1787–88 is not the weakness and disunity but the political strength of Antifederalism. That large numbers of Americans could actually reject a plan of government created by a body 'composed of the first characters in the Continent' and backed by Washington and nearly the whole of the natural aristocracy of the country said more about the changing character of American politics and society in the eighties than did the Constitution's eventual acceptance." Gordon S. Wood, *The Creation of the American Republic, 1776–1787* (New York: Norton, 1969), pp. 498–99.

25. Herbert J. Storing, ed., *The Complete Anti-Federalists* (Chicago: University of Chicago Press, 1981), vol. 1, p. 22.

26. Storing, *Anti-Federalists*, p. 23. Storing noted that the

> Anti-Federalist position was not so much that government ought to foster religion as that the consolidating Constitution threatened the healthy religious situation as it then existed.

The religious diversity of the whole United States seemed so great as to strain to breaking point any publicly useful religious foundation for the nation as a whole. Consolidation would require, then, substituting for religion some other foundation of political morality—which the Anti-Federalists foresaw would be an aggregate of selfish interests held together by force. This feuding would be strengthened by the absence from the Constitution of any religious test for office holding, which seemed intended to further undermine the public significance of religious conviction.

27. There were also numerous Antifederalists who had no special concern for individual rights but who seized on them as a potent issue they could use to attack a federal government they opposed for a variety of personal, political, economic or other reasons. Patrick Henry is probably the archetype for this group.

28. Storing, *Anti-Federalists*, p. 664.

29. Bernard Schwartz refers to evidence that the Philadelphia newspapers did not reach Boston in time to influence the proposals, a fact seen by Antifederalists as the result of a Federalist conspiracy in the post office. Schwartz, *Bill of Rights*, vol. 2, p. 674. For a fuller discussion, see Schwartz, *Bill of Rights*, vol. 2, pp. 674–728.

30. Schwartz, *Bill of Rights*, vol. 2, p. 712.

31. As were most Baptists in New England, Backus was wary of a strong central authority, according to historian William McLoughlin. William G. McLoughlin, ed., *Isaac Backus on Church, State and Calvinism, Pamphlets, 1754–1789* (Cambridge, Mass.: Harvard University Press, 1968). McLoughlin also notes that Backus was at first reluctant to accept this post. In his diary Backus wrote, "I thought I should not go, but as religious liberty is concerned in the affair, and many were earnest for my going, I consented." Quoted in William G. McLoughlin, *New England Dissent 1630–1883: The Baptists and the Separation of Church and State* (Cambridge, Mass.: Harvard University Press, 1971), vol. 2, pp. 782–83. McLoughlin also points out that "one of the most inexplicable aspects of the ratifying convention in Massachusetts is that none of the over twenty Baptist delegates appears to have suggested an amendment to the constitution to guarantee that Congress would not interfere with religious liberty" vol. 2, p. 783.

32. McLoughlin, *New England Dissent*, p. 15, citing Backus's speech in Elliot's *Debates*.

33. Schwartz, *Bill of Rights*, vol. 2, p. 735.

34. Ibid., p. 757.

35. Antieau, Downey, and Roberts, *Freedom*, p. 117, quoting the *New Haven Gazette*, December 4, 1788.

36. Ibid., pp. 117–18.

37. Schwartz, *Bill of Rights*, vol. 2, p. 761.

38. Ibid., p. 796. In his well-known essay numbered 10 among the *Federalist Papers*, Madison rails against the "dangerous vice" of faction, which he defined as "a number of citizens . . . who are united and actuated by some common impulse of passion, or of interest, adverse to the rights of other citizens, or to the permanent and aggregate interests of the community." As to religion, Madison noted, "A religious sect may degenerate into a political faction in a part of the Confederacy; but the variety of sects dispersed over the entire fact of it must secure the national councils against any danger from that source." Clinton Rossiter, ed., *The Federalist Papers* (New York: New American Library, 1961), pp. 77–78, 84.

39. Ibid., pp. 796–97.

40. Schwartz, *Bill of Rights*, vol. 2, p. 842.

41. The only difference between the two is that the later document pronounces that "all men have an equal, natural and unalienable right to the free exercise of religion" while the Virginia Declaration simply asserts that "all men are equally entitled to the free exercise of religion."

42. Quoted in Robert S. Alley, ed., *James Madison: A Free Conscience in a Secular Republic* (New York: Prometheus Press, 1985) p. 51.

43. Curry, however, argues that the Founding Fathers made no distinction between this nonpreferential language and an absolute prohibition of establishment. "Thus, men unmistakably opposed to proposals for non-discriminatory government assistance to religion continued to use the concept of preference for one religion." Curry, *The First Freedoms*, p. 212.

44. Schwartz, *Bill of Rights*, vol. 2, p. 912. There is little recorded debate on each of the dozens of proposals. It is worth noting, however, that Antifederalist Thomas Tredwell specifically cited religion as one area in which the people need to be protected from the federal government. He proclaimed at the convention, "I could have wished also that sufficient caution had been used to secure to us our religious liberties, and to have prevented the general government from tyrannizing over our consciences by a religious establishment—a tyranny of all others most dreadful, and which will assuredly be exercised whenever it shall be thought necessary for the promotion and support of their political measures." vol. 2, p. 864.

45. Ibid., p. 977. Writing to James Madison in 1789, William R. Davie noted that the "farrago of amendments borrowed from Virginia is by no means to be considered the sense of this country; they were proposed amidst the violence and confusion of party heat, at a critical moment in our Convention, and adopted by the opposition without one moment's consideration." But he also said that "a constitutional guarantee for the free exercise of . . . religion" was on the short list of important amendments sought by "the honest and serious." Ibid., p. 980.

46. Ibid., p. 983, citing Judge Dumbauld.

47. Rhode Island did not ratify the Constitution until 1790, the year after Congress approved the establishment clause. In ratifying, it issued a declaration of principles that included a nonestablishment clause virtually identical to the ones offered several years before by Virginia, North Carolina, and New York. See Stokes, *Church and State*, vol. 1, pp. 609–10. This action obviously had no impact on the first Congress' establishment clause deliberations. Levy calls it a "superfluous flourish which had no effect on the framing of the First Amendment." Levy, *Establishment*, p. 73.

48. The House debates are recorded in Joseph Gales and W. W. Seaton, eds., *The Debates and Proceedings in the Congress of the United States, Compiled from Authentic Materials*, 42 vols. (Washington, D.C. 1834–56), vol. 1, p. 451, generally referred to as the *Annals of Congress* ("*Annals*"). For a brief discussion on sources, see Levy, *Establishment*, pp. 187–89. See also Marion Tinling, "Thomas Lloyd's Reports of the First Federal Congress," *William and Mary Quarterly*, 3rd ser., 18 (October 1961): 519–45.

49. Gales and Seaton, *Annals*, p. 451.

50. Gales and Seaton, *Annals*, p. 452.

51. Gales and Seaton, *Annals*, p. 757. It is interesting to note that Library of

Congress archivist James Hutson has recently unearthed a draft bill of rights written by Roger Sherman of Connecticut. Sherman's draft, which contained eleven enumerated amendments to the Constitution, was dated "July 1789," a month after Madison's proposals to Congress. Although Sherman adopted some of Madison's proposals verbatim, he left out any form of antiestablishment clause. As to freedom of religion, he wrote: "The people have certain natural rights which are retained by them when they enter into Society, Such are the rights of Conscience in matters of religion." "Handwritten Bill of Rights Found," *New York Times*, July 29, 1987, pp. A1, C21.

52. Gales and Seaton, *Annals*, p. 757.

53. Was Sherman, representing a state with a strong "Standing Order," being a little disingenuous? Under strict Federalist theory, the central government was powerless to impinge on any areas not expressly mentioned in the Constitution. Yet Sherman himself circulated a draft bill of rights that included numerous provisions technically unnecessary under the Federalist scheme. See "Handwritten Bill," pp. A1, C21.

54. Gales and Seaton, *Annals*, pp. 757–58.

55. Ibid., p. 758.

56. Ibid.

57. Ibid., pp. 758–59.

58. Ibid., p. 759.

59. Ibid.

60. Ibid., pp. 783–84.

61. Ibid., p. 796.

62. Linda Grant DePauw, ed., *Documentary History of the First Federal Congress of the United States of America* (Baltimore: Johns Hopkins University Press, 1977–), vol. 1, pp. 137–38.

63. Ibid.

64. Ibid., p. 151.

65. Ibid., p. 166.

66. See, for example, Antieau, Downey, and Roberts, *Freedom*, p. 133.

67. DePauw, *First Federal Congress*, vol. 1, pp. 182, 186, 189, 199 and vol. 3, p. 228.

68. Massachusetts, Connecticut, and Georgia waited until 1839 to ratify the Bill of Rights. Virginia, which ratified it in 1791, provides us with the only record of debates on the establishment clause. Eight Virginia Senators who opposed the First Amendment said:

> The 3d does not prohibit the rights of conscience from being violated or infringed: and although it goes to restrain Congress from passing laws establishing any national religion, they might, notwithstanding, levy taxes to any amount, for the support of religion or its preachers; and any particular denomination of Christians might be so favored and supported by the General Government, as to give it a decided advantage over others, and in process of time render it as powerful and dangerous as if it was established as the national religion of the country. . . . This amendment then, when considered as it relates to any of the rights it is pretended to secure, will be found totally inadequate.

Quoted in Levy, *Judgments*, p. 188. See *Journal of the Senate of the Commonwealth of Virginia, Begun and Held in the City of Richmond, on Monday, the 18th of*

October . . . 1789 (Richmond, 1828), p. 62. For obvious reasons this has been cited favorably by accommodationist scholars; see, for example, Corwin, "The Supreme Court as National School Board," *Law and Contemporary Problems* 14 (Winter 1949), p. 12. Levy points out that the eight Senators had a history of *supporting* religious establishment in Virginia. He thus concludes that these statements were merely a political ploy by Antifederalists seeking to use any argument to attack the Constitution. See Levy, *Judgments*, pp. 188–90 and *Establishment*, pp. 85–89. Patrick Henry, who was the prime opponent of Madison and Jefferson in their disestablishmentarian efforts in Virginia, made a similar about-face when he thought he could make political points by attacking the Constitution for failing to adequately protect religious liberty.

69. Stokes, *Church and State*, vol. 1, p. 543. See Michael J. Malbin, *Religion and Politics: The Intentions of the Authors of the First Amendment* (Washington, D.C.: American Enterprise Institute, 1978).

70. Joseph Story, *Commentaries on the Constitution* (1833), section 1879.

71. Malbin, *Religion and Politics*, p. 14.

72. Ibid. See also Walter F. Berns, *The First Amendment and the Future of American Democracy* (New York: Basic Books, 1976), pp. 8–9.

73. Thomas John Curry, *The First Freedoms: Church and State in America to the Passage of the First Amendment* (New York: Oxford University Press, 1986), p. 222.

74. Ibid.

75. Robert Cord, *Separation of Church and State: Historical Fact and Current Fiction* (New York: Lambeth Press, 1982), pp. 47, 49.

76. Levy, *Establishment*, p. 221.

3

CHURCH AND STATE UNDER THE ESTABLISHMENT CLAUSE: THE FIRST 150 YEARS

Less than twenty-four hours after adopting the First Amendment's prohibitions on laws respecting an establishment of religion, the Congress decided to express its thanks to God Almighty for the many blessings enjoyed by the new nation. On motion by Boudinot, the legislative body requested that the president "recommend to the people . . . a day of public thanksgiving and prayer, to be observed by acknowledging, with grateful hearts, the many signal favors of God," especially in that He gave them the opportunity to establish the Constitution.[1]

Only two members of Congress rose to speak against the motion. Burke did not like "this mimicking of European customs, where they made a mere mockery of thanksgivings," but seemed to have no concerns about Congress's authority to involve itself in matters of religion. His colleague, Tucker, voiced that objection among several others, however. "[I]t is a religious matter," he asserted, "and, as such, is proscribed to us." But his principal concern seemed to be an uncertainty about whether the people would want to give thanks for a constitution "until they have experienced that it promotes their safety and happiness." Perhaps, he suggested, if there must be a day of thanksgiving, "let it be done by the . . . States; they know best what reason their constituents have to be pleased with the establishment of this Constitution."[2]

Apparently sidestepping Tucker's establishment clause concerns, Congressmen Sherman and Boudinot cited the salutary effect of thanksgivings throughout Western history, and the motion passed without further recorded discussion.[3] And so, probably before the ink on the establishment clause had fully dried, the Congress adopted a proposal clearly promoting religious activities with hardly a wave in the First Amendment's direction. This was merely the first day of a 150 year period during which most of America—especially the government—simply ignored the establishment clause altogether. Only in the last 40 years have we thought much about the clause, and only since the early 1960s has the "separation of church and state" become not only a cardinal tenet of the American creed in any practical sense but also the subject of virtually continuous federal litigation.

Commentators on the establishment clause have tended to follow this pattern, typically skipping from the late-eighteenth century to the mid-twentieth, picking up only a few scattered pieces of history along the way. The parts of church-state lore that are highlighted depend primarily on the commentator's point of view. Strict separationists generally focus on Madison's "Detached Memoranda,"[4] written late in life, in which he decried the days of prayer and fasting he had earlier declared as president, and, of course, Thomas Jefferson's famous letter to the Danbury Baptist Association in 1802, proclaiming that the First Amendment "built a wall of separation between Church and State."[5] Then they usually skip to the *Reynolds* case—not for its holding under the free exercise clause but for its invocation of Madison and Jefferson to interpret the religion clauses of the First Amendment—and on to *Everson*, the beginning of the modern establishment clause era. Once again, this is not for the case's decision that states may bus children to parochial schools, but for the strict separationist rhetoric resounding through both majority and dissenting opinions. And, finally, *Engel* and *Schempp* stand as the flagship cases in the strict separationist armada.

Not surprisingly, accommodationists tend to recite a different litany. They too start with the framers, but they prefer to focus on acts rather than words. So Madison's declarations of thanksgiving days are seen as more important than his later disavowal of them, and Jefferson's decision to send federal aid to religious schools and missions for the Kaskaskia Indians are better sources of framers' intentions than a private letter to one particular Baptist group.[6] And the Northwest Ordinance of 1787 provided that the government should promote "religion, morality and knowledge" as they were all necessary to good government and happiness.[7] The next stop is Justice Joseph Story, appointed to the Supreme Court by James Madison, whose influential *Commentaries on the Constitution* proclaimed that "[p]robably at the time of the adoption of the constitution, and of the [first] amendment to it, . . . the general if not the universal, sentiment in America was that Christianity ought to receive encouragement from the State, so far as was not incompatible with the private rights of religious worship."[8]

Not only should Christianity be encouraged by the state, but, as Story went on to say, "Any attempt to level all religions, and to make it a state policy to hold all in utter indifference, would have created universal disapprobation, if not universal indignation."[9] After Story, accommodationists typically jump to the adoption of the Fourteenth Amendment and point out that there is no convincing evidence supporting the Court's holding that the religion clauses of the First Amendment were thereby made binding upon the states. And for modern support, they invoke not only the Court's references to "benevolent neutrality" but also Justice Douglas's oft-quoted dictum: "We are a religious people whose institutions presuppose a Supreme Being."[10]

While this battle of the proof-texts has done relatively little to give us a broad contextual sense of the relationship of church and state in America, it has been instrumental in the development of existing establishment clause jurisprudence and in the many calls for new and better approaches.[11] The most remarkable aspect of both sides' postconstitutional history, however, is not the evidence itself but the lack of it. For well over a century, the establishment clause lay essentially dormant because the relationship of church and state was virtually never a federal issue. As we saw in the first chapter, the Supreme Court's major contribution to church-state relations was its clear signal in cases such as *Reynolds* and *Davis v. Beason* that "[w]hilst legislation for the establishment of religion is forbidden, and its free exercise permitted, it does not follow that everything that may be so called can be tolerated."[12] Mormons were not the only group to have their religious liberties legislatively limited during this period. Not only did blasphemy laws stay on the books for many years, but blacks in the nineteenth century were prohibited from preaching except on their masters' property and then only if whites were present.[13] If nothing else, the Supreme Court clearly stated that it would not offer refuge for the protection of those falling outside the religious mainstream.

Despite the paucity of federal cases on church-state matters, state and local church-state issues abounded.[14] It would take several volumes to chronicle the relationship of religion and government during this period properly, but we should, nevertheless, take note of the patterns and problems making up that history.

For example, in the late-eighteenth and early-nineteenth centuries, laws and constitutional provisions promoting established churches in the various states were eliminated. This was not, however, the result of some national disestablishmentarian movement of which the establishment clause of the First Amendment was a part. The disestablishment of state churches resulted from myriad political, economic, sociological, and religious factors that operated most strongly on state and local levels. Revivalism, pluralism, the Enlightenment, anticlericalism, the Revolutionary War (in the South), the rise of Unitarianism (in the North), and a simple aversion to tax paying fueled the fires of disestablishment, and ultimately the generally conservative, weakened establishments gave way.[15] But disestablishment of state churches was not the result of a successful onslaught directed at a monolithic institution; to the contrary, the churches lost their support because they were unable to muster enough political power to preserve it.

Although state supported churches had become less powerful, disestablishment had an impact on the lives of at least some Americans at the time—ministers of previously established churches had a new set of problems,[16] and the states had to learn to deal with religious corporations that did not fit neatly in the predominantly English jurisprudence America had inherited.[17] The issue of the extent to which religious organizations could be incorporated under state law gave rise to the Supreme Court's one foray into local church-state disputes. In *Terrett v. Taylor*, the Court reviewed an 1801 Virginia law claiming the right to all of the property of the Episcopal churches in the state and directing that some of the land be sold and the proceeds used for the benefit of the poor.[18] The 1801 law conflicted with a number of earlier statutes that the legislature argued were "inconsistent with the principles of the [Virginia] constitution and religious freedom."[19]

Justice Story's opinion argued that "[i]t is difficult to perceive how the legislature may not enact laws more effectually to enable all sects to accomplish the great objects of religion by giving them corporate rights for the management of their property."[20] Although the Virginia legislature could not permit "a religious establishment which should have exclusive rights and prerogatives, or compel the citizens to worship under a stipulated form or discipline, to pay taxes to those whose creed they could not conscientiously believe," Justice Story asserted that "[t]he free exercise of religion cannot be justly deemed to be restrained by aiding with equal attention the votaries of every sect to perform their own religious duties, or by establishing funds for the support of ministers, for public charities, for the endowment of churches, or for the sepultures of the dead."[21] He then concluded that it was not contrary to the Virginia Constitution for the legislature to create religious corporations with the power to own and manage property; therefore, the state of Virginia was not entitled to seize the lands belonging to the churches.

In taking note of the disappearance of state churches, we should not believe that disestablishmentarianism signaled either disdain for churches generally or even restiveness with the nation's Christian heritage. Quite to the contrary, Americans throughout the early national period enjoyed constant outpourings of revivalism and the rapid growth of evangelically oriented churches and voluntary associations. At the same time, few doubted the country's divine destiny or its fundamental relationship with Christianity. What emerged as the country approached the nineteenth century was the "era of republican Protestantism" in which much of the populace shared "a vision of the United States as a protestant Christian nation conformed to the divine will, not through a formal . . . establishment of religion, but through a common life renewed by evangelical religion and thus spontaneously God oriented."[22]

The Northwest Ordinance of 1787 proclaimed, "religion, morality and knowledge [were] necessary to good government and the happiness of mankind," and vast numbers of Americans believed just that. More important for our interest in the relationship of law to religion, judges rarely saw the formal disestablishment of state churches as any impediment to enforcing laws protecting or supporting Christianity in general. In addition to Justice Story's proclamations discussed above, New York's Chief Justice James Kent announced in *People v. Ruggles* (1811) that the "people of this state, in common with the people of this country, professed doctrines of Christianity as the rule of their faith and practice."[23] In fact, the most noteworthy aspect of church-state litigation in the first half of the nineteenth century was that there really was none to speak of. A couple of accused blasphemers challenged blasphemy laws to no avail; but otherwise, the courts were remarkably quiet.[24]

Cases dealing with church-state matters increased sharply in the latter part of the nineteenth century, when immigration, industrialization, and a host of other factors challenged the Protestant hegemony. Sunday laws, which fundamentally dated back to a proclamation of the Emperor Constantine in 321 A.D., existed throughout the United States from the earliest colonial days and survived unthreatened until mid-century.[25] From 1846 to 1887, the *American Digest* reports eighteen decisions dealing with Sunday closing laws, and in only one, an 1858 California case, did the court find the legislation unconstitutional on religious freedom grounds.[26] In the remaining seventeen cases, including two subsequent California cases, judges uniformly upheld the sanctity of the Lord's day.[27] Although some of the cases purported to rely on the pagan origins of Sunday laws (which recognized the god of the sun), the laws themselves made it clear that "all Sunday legislation from Constantine to William Penn was based on the supposition that the Lord's day is the divinely appointed Sabbath and [the laws were] enacted to preserve the day from desecration."[28] Although a few court decisions held Sunday laws unconstitutional, by and large the practice was upheld as, in the words of the Supreme Court of Iowa in 1848, "a time-honored and heaven-appointed institution."[29] By the 1930s, public referenda and legislative action had eliminated a number of Sunday laws, but few were determined by a court to be unconstitutional establishments of religion under federal or state constitutions.[30]

By mid-century, a much more inflammatory church-state controversy emerged: The public schools began to provoke not only violent confrontations inspired by religious conflict and nativism but also the litigation that remains unabated today. Even the issues, prayer and Bible reading, are unchanged. Perhaps more than any other aspect of church-state relations, the abiding concern over the link between religion and public education should provide a useful lens through which we can view trends and patterns in church-state relationships during the 150 years the establishment clause lay fallow.

For virtually all of our history as a nation, and certainly throughout the nineteenth century, the public schools have, in most communities, been under the control of a Protestant majority that has seen Bible reading as part of the nondenominational Christian faith that is a bulwark of American society.[31] Christianizing both America and the world (in a Protestant manner, of course) was high on the cultural agenda during the early part of the nineteenth century when our system of broad-based public education developed, and the schools were widely seen as the crucible in which morals—a concept virtually inextricably linked to religion—would be ground into the character of American youth. As historian Timothy Smith has noted, "By the middle of the nineteenth century, leading citizens assumed that Americanism and Protestantism were synonyms and that education and Protestantism were allies."[32] Even Horace Mann, far more liberal in religious matters than the thousands of school boards across the country, urged Bible reading in the schools to support the development of morality.[33] Yet by the middle of the century, religious diversity, most often in the form of Roman Catholic and Jewish immigration, set the stage for several legal challenges to the established practice.

Two of the earliest cases arose in New England, where a link between Protestant Christianity and education dated back to the Puritans. In 1854, a Maine court declared that a regulation requiring that a Protestant version of the Bible be read in the public schools was consistent with Maine's constitutional guarantee of religious freedom. An 1866 Massachusetts court confirmed that a school may expel a student for refusing to bow his head during the school's opening prayer.[34] Most of the other controversies took place in the expanding Western states, where religious and ethnic pluralism was as much a tradition as republican Protestantism. An Iowa court in 1884, for example, upheld legislation providing that "the Bible shall not be excluded from any school . . . nor shall any pupil be required to read it, contrary to the wishes of his guardian" despite the state's constitutional prohibition on religious establishments.[35] On the other hand, in 1890, a Wisconsin court declared that Bible reading in the public schools was impermissible even if objecting students [were] permitted to leave, since it would "tend to destroy the equality and uniformity of treatment of the pupils sought to be established and protected by the constitution."[36]

Perhaps the best known of the nineteenth-century cases involving religion in the schools took place in Cincinnati, Ohio, and historian Robert Michaelsen has provided us with a detailed account of the case and its context.[37] In the late 1860s, Cincinnati was, in Michaelsen's words, "one of the most [religiously] heterogenous cities in the United States. . . . On the four corners of the busy intersection of Eighth and Plum Streets there stood the city building, the Catholic cathedral, Temple Benai Yeshurun, and the 'new and radical Unitarian Church'—with a Presbyterian church standing right next to it."[38] In 1869, the school board decided to abandon the practice of reading the Scriptures in the public schools, thus bringing about "The Cincinnati Bible War." Opponents of the board's action filed suit for an injunction, which was granted by the superior court on the grounds that "Christianity was 'the prevailing religion of the State.' "[39] Ultimately, the Ohio Supreme Court reversed, asserting that the Ohio constitution did "not enjoin or require religious instruction, or the reading of religious books, in the public schools," but that the lower court had no right to interfere with a school board's decision.[40]

Professor Michaelsen has summarized the views of both sides in the Bible War, and they stand as remarkably good examples of positions on religion in the public schools, not only in the nineteenth century but also in the twentieth. Rufus King, attorney for the plaintiffs, who had been a student of Joseph Story's at Harvard, posited that "since there was no established church in the United States the public school was 'the only means left' in which 'the simple tenets of political religion' could be spread."[41] Unitarian minister A. D. Mayo joined the "common religion" cause as well, arguing that the "public religion" was nonsectarian, and the common school must acknowledge "the universal obligation to worship God, and do good to man, as the condition of republican life."[42] On the other side, Judge J. B. Stallo, an attorney for the school board, and, according to Michaelsen, "probably the widest read man in the city if not the whole West,"[43] declared that the state was "as godless as a steam engine" with " 'all forms of belief and unbelief' possessing equal rights."[44] Similarly, Presbyterian elder and lawyer Stanley Mathews "found the 'broad Christianity' " of the so-called common religion to be "nothing more than 'broad humbug.' "[45] For Mathews, "religion could 'stand on its own legs,' and if it could not, 'then it ought not.' "[46] Rabbi Wise joined the debate, asserting that " 'the state has no religion' and the public schools must be 'secular.' "[47] Although the secular forces won the disposition of the case, the Supreme Court would not go as far as to declare Bible reading in public schools unacceptable. Rather, it merely protected the right of the local board of education to make the decision as to whether religion would be practiced in the schools.

Turn-of-the-century commentator Samuel W. Brown determined that between 1850 and 1912 "the supreme courts of no less than twenty-one states [were] called upon to decide at least thirty cases involving in some form the question of the proper relation of religion and public education."[48] By Brown's count, "seventeen cases, in fifteen states, [were] decided in favor of the secular view" while "thirteen cases, in nine states, in favor of the religious view."[49] But, as historian Michaelsen has observed, Brown generally equated "religious" with "sectarian," and thus the "secular view" court decisions may have struck down particular sectarian practices in the school but did not necessarily eradicate all religious practices such as school prayers or Bible reading.[50]

The public school and the Bible maintained their close relationship at the opening of the twentieth century, with three-quarters of school districts surveyed reporting regular Bible reading.[51] And while only one state law required that the Scriptures be read in the school in 1900, by the 1930s the number had increased to thirteen, and then to thirty-seven by 1950 (with only seven prohibiting such Bible reading).[52] The District of Columbia presents a particularly interesting case. Political scientist Alvin W. Johnson pointed out in 1934 that "Bible reading in the District of Columbia is controlled by the federal constitution and amendments [including the establishment clause]." Johnson noted not only that the Bible was read in all of the district's schools but also that the board of education issued a regulation in 1926 mandating that "teacher[s] shall, as a part of the opening exercises, read, without note or comment, a portion of the bible, repeat the Lord's Prayer and conduct appropriate singing by the pupils."[53] Thus even where the establishment clause directly governed the local public schools, it did not appear to bar prayer and Bible reading. And elsewhere, the federal Constitution and courts had no jurisdiction. As of 1934, Johnson had no hesitation in stating that "[t]he power to regulate Bible reading in the public school does not appear among the list of powers delegated to the federal government by the constitution of the United States" and therefore the establishment clause of the First Amendment "cannot be invoked to protect the citizens of the respective states."[54]

Although the trend towards legislation requiring Bible reading could be seen as evidence of growing support for school devotionals, it may well signal increasing opposition instead. As long as local school districts were firmly controlled by an effective mainstream hegemony, there would be no need for state legislation. Inevitably, with greater diversity on the local level came greater dissent. In several cases in the late-nineteenth and early-twentieth centuries, for example, Roman Catholics successfully brought suit to have Bible reading in the schools declared improper.[55] Thus the Protestant voting majority asserted its legislative control and acted by statute, and at least as of the 1930s, the state courts universally concluded that this type of legislation, even when it specified the use of the King James Bible, did not constitute "sectarian" activities in contravention of state constitutions.[56]

Bible reading was not the only church-state issue in the public school at the dawn of this century. As the Supreme Court cases of the last few decades have shown, issues such as released-time religious education, Darwinism versus creationism, Ten Commandment–based morality lessons, and a handful of others became the focus for a nation that continued to see public education as a critical element (perhaps *the* critical element) in Americanizing the native and foreign born alike. As all of the school cases and statutes demonstrate, Americans at the state and local level have consistently encouraged "nondenominational" piety, and even today vast numbers of this nation's citizens support prayers and Bible reading in the schools.

As a result, the nineteenth-century arguments over devotionals and Bible reading in the public schools ring with a great deal of familiarity even today. Local school boards and state educational authorities continue to struggle with the desires of some parents to have their children take part in public school devotionals and the vigorous opposition of other parents. For the first 150 years of the republic, these difficult matters were resolved on the state and local level with the wide spectrum of results inevitably spawned by the specific needs and concerns of individual communities. Since the Supreme Court decided in the twentieth century to make the establishment clause binding on the states, however, jurisdiction over church-state issues has largely been a national rather than a local issue.

Reading history as taught by modern Supreme Court cases, we are tempted to think this national approach was adopted during the nineteenth century when the Fourteenth Amendment was added to the Constitution. But this is not the case; church-state controversy did not become a truly national issue until the middle of the twentieth century. Not until *Cantwell v. Connecticut* in 1940 did the Supreme Court bring the dictates of the religion clauses of the First Amendment to bear on the states, and the establishment clause was first applied to state action in 1947 in *Everson v. Board of Education*. *Cantwell* and *Everson* were part of a line of cases in which certain provisions of the Bill of Rights were "incorporated" in the due process clause of the Fourteenth Amendment. Then, in *Adamson v. California* (1947), Justice Black, in a dissenting opinion, posited that one of the primary objectives of the Fourteenth Amendment was to make all of the provisions of the Bill of Rights applicable to the states.[57]

The issue of whether any or all of the constitutional guarantees in the Bill of Rights are incorporated in the Fourteenth Amendment has been widely debated by scholars of history and law, and there is no need to revisit that controversy at length.[58] Essentially, historian Charles Fairman and others have countered that "the record of history is overwhelmingly against" Justice Black's conclusion, and even Leonard Levy, who certainly believes that the First Amendment *should* be binding on the states through the Fourteenth Amendment, whether or not its framers intended such a result, has awarded victory in the historical debate to Fairman.[59] Suffice it to say that there is scant evidence supporting the theory that the Bill of Rights was intended by the Congress and ratifying states to be incorporated in toto in the Fourteenth Amendment, and there is no evidence strong enough to support the conclusion that the Congress specifically intended to resolve the growing number of church-state disputes around the country by granting all Americans the right not to be deprived of life, liberty, or property without due process of law.

One nineteenth-century church-state controversy that the federal government almost did address was the issue of aid to religious schools. As we have seen, the public schools were strongly influenced by Protestant attitudes and piety. Frequently, not only were prayers and the reading of the King James Bible included in schooling but also the texts used for ostensibly secular instruction were often less than kind to "Papists" and other religious minorities. For this and other reasons, Roman Catholic immigrants became dedicated to building parochial schools and sought to share the governmental largess appropriated for the public school system—yet another church-state issue enduring to the present.

Following the lead of President Grant, Congressman James G. Blaine proposed in 1875 that the Constitution of the United States be amended to provide that no tax funds shall be used for the "support of any school . . . under the control of any religious or anti-religious sect, organization, or denomination, or wherein the particular creed or tenets shall be read or taught."[60] In 1876, this amendment was overwhelmingly adopted by the House of Representatives, but the Senate sought to add some protection for the prevailing patterns of Protestant piety in the schools, and the words "This article shall not be construed to prohibit a reading of the Bible in any school or institution" were added. The vote was considerably closer in the Senate: twenty-eight in favor, sixteen opposed, and twenty-seven not voting. The abstentions prevented the amendment from being adopted by the requisite two-thirds, and, after several more attempts, the Blaine Amendment dropped from the congressional agenda.[61]

Although the federal government failed to resolve this nineteenth-century parochial school aid issue, the states took decisive action. In the thirty-six years between 1877 and 1913, thirty-three states adopted constitutional amendments proscribing aid to religious schools.[62] Exactly what constituted improper aid to church-related schools was, nevertheless, a difficult issue. While taxes could not be levied directly in support of religious schools, courts issued differing opinions as to whether public school buildings could be used for religious purposes and what kind of supplies, such as textbooks, could be made available to private school students.[63] The federal court litigation of the last few decades well testifies to the difficulty of these questions; they certainly have not been simplified by either state or federal constitutional adjudications.

The schools, of course, were not the only places where religion and the republic have intersected over the last 200 years. We have set aside countless official days of prayer and thanksgiving observances, we still swear oaths on a Bible, pledge allegiance to "one nation under God," affirm our trust in the deity every time we make or receive a cash payment, and hire clergy to pray over our legislatures. Many of these practices antedate the Constitution while more recent ones simply serve to reaffirm the fact that most Americans throughout our history have seen God and country as inextricably linked.

We can thus see the nineteenth-century struggles as representative of many of the same conflicts that persist in late-twentieth-century America as a Protestant majority struggles to deal with the burden of religious pluralism. And we can also see that the Supreme Court has taken very much of a minority view in terms of eighteenth- and nineteenth-century judicial decisions when it has struck down Bible reading and numerous other governmentally sponsored practices supporting religious activity. There is nothing fundamentally wrong in that; in fact, constitutional history abounds with examples of the United States Supreme Court finding rights in the federal Constitution that state courts had not otherwise located. But to attack school prayer and Bible reading is to strike deeply at the heart of Americans' cultural self-understanding. To afford all Americans their constitutional rights under the establishment clause without at the same time appearing hostile to vital cultural linchpins requires a carefully constructed and well defined First Amendment jurisprudence. It is not clear that the Supreme Court has yet accomplished that goal, and the next chapter will attempt to provide a useful framework for the task.

NOTES

1. Joseph Gales and W. W. Seaton, eds., *The Debates and Proceedings in the Congress of the United States, Compiled from Authentic Materials* (Annals), 42 vols. (Washington, D.C., 1834–1856), vol. 1, p. 949–50.

2. Ibid.

3. Ibid.

4. Elizabeth Fleet, ed., "Madison's 'Detached Memoranda,' " *William and Mary Quarterly*, 3 (1946), pp. 535ff.

5. The letter is reproduced in John F. Wilson and Donald L. Drakeman, eds., *Church and State in American History: The Burden of Religious Pluralism* (Boston: Beacon Press, 1987), pp. 78–79.

6. See Robert L. Cord, *Separation of Church and State: Historical Fact and Current Fiction* (New York: Lambeth Press, 1982), pp. 34–47. Jefferson sent to the Senate for advice and consent a proposed treaty with the Kaskaskia Indians providing that "the United States will give annually for seven years one hundred dollars towards the support of a priest of [the Roman Catholic] religion. . . . And the United States will further give the sum of three hundred dollars to assist the said tribe in the erection of a church." Richard Peters, ed., *The Public Statutes at Large of the United States in America*, vol. 7 (Boston: Little and Brown, 1848), p. 79, quoted in Robert Cord, *Separation of Church and State: Historical Fact and Current Fiction* (New York: Lambeth Press, 1982), p. 79.

7. Quoted in Leonard W. Levy, *The Establishment Clause* (New York: Macmillan, 1986), p. 173–74.

8. Joseph Story, *Commentaries on the Constitution of the United States*, 3 vols. (Boston: Hillard, Gray, 1833), pp. 722ff. Quoted in Wilson and Drakeman, *Church and State*, pp. 92–93.

9. Ibid.

10. See Zorach v. Clauson, 343 U.S. 306 (1952).

11. By and large, the strict separationists have won the battle of rhetoric: the separation of church and state is clearly a part of our national vocabulary, and virtually all establishment clause cases begin with an almost ritualistic appeal to that fundamental concept. But the accommodationists, have, with the exception of school prayer and some forms of aid to parochial schools, won the war: our money and flag salute proclaim God's relationship with the republic, each year we as a nation celebrate Christmas and Thanksgiving as well as a National Day of Prayer, our taxes pay for chaplains to minister to the Congress and the military, and now, it appears, the Supreme Court is aligned to interpret the establishment clause even more narrowly than in the past.

12. Davis v. Beason, 133 U.S. 333 at 345 (1890).

13. See Leonard W. Levy, *Treason Against God: A History of the Offense of Blasphemy* (New York: Schocken Books, 1981). On the slave codes, see, for example, Kenneth W. Stampp, *The Peculiar Institution: Slavery in the Ante-Bellum South* (New York: Random House, 1956), p. 208; Eugene D. Genovese, *Roll, Jordan, Roll: The World the Slaves Made* (New York: Random House, 1972), p. 257; see also William Goodell, *The American Slave Code* (New York: American and Foreign Anti-Slavery Society, 1853).

14. Efforts to make local church-state issues into federal cases were rebuffed by the Supreme Court. In Permoli v. New Orleans, 3 How. 589, 11 L.Ed. 739 (1845), for example, the Supreme Court was asked to invalidate a New Orleans ordinance prohibiting any Roman Catholic churches from exposing corpses. Permoli, who was fined $50 for officiating at a funeral in which a corpse was exposed, argued that the ordinance violated the free exercise clause of the United States Constitution. The Court held that it had no jurisdiction, saying, "The Constitution makes no provision for protecting the citizens of the respective states in their religious liberties; this is left to the State constitutions and laws: nor is there any inhibition imposed by the Constitution of the United States in respect of the States." 3 How. at 609, 11 L.Ed. at 748. See also Barron v. Baltimore, 32 U.S. 242, 7 Pet. 243 (1833).

15. Lyman Beecher, Connecticut minister and supporter of that state's established church, had a different picture of his disestablishmentarian opponents: "nearly all the minor sects, besides the Sabbath-breakers, rum-selling tippling folks, infidels, and ruff-scuff generally." Quoted in Edwin S. Gaustad, *Faith of Our Fathers: Religion and the New Nation* (San Francisco: Harper & Row, 1987), p. 120. The "ruff-scuff" prevailed in 1818 by a vote of 13,918 to 12,364. Ibid. See also, William G. McLoughlin, *New England Dissent, 1630–1833* (Cambridge, Mass.: Harvard University Press, 1971) and Franklin Hamlin Littell, *From State Church to Pluralism: A Protestant Interpretation of Religion in American History* (New York: Macmillan, 1971), chapter 2.

16. See, for example, Ann Douglas, *The Feminization of American Culture* (New York: Avon Books, 1977), chapter 1.

17. See, for example, Weld v. May, 63 Mass. (9 Such.) 181 (1852) (Congrega-

tional church is not a corporation.); Bean v. Christian Church, 61 N.H. 260 (1881) (Trustees, deacons, and similar officers of an unincorporated church are a corporation for holding real and personal property.); and other cases collected in the *American Digest, Centennial Edition* 42, columns 1420–30, 1435–36. Several states had statutes or constitutional provisions prohibiting the incorporation of churches. This created confusion when the churches tried to take title to property. In Pennsylvania, an 1855 law required that churches' charters grant the laity control over the disposal of property. See Christ's Evangelical Lutheran Church of Beaver Falls, 5 Pa.Co.Ct.R. 121 (1886).

18. Terrett v. Taylor, 9 Cranch 43, 3 L.Ed. 650 (1815).

19. 9 Cranch at 48, 3 L.Ed. at 652.

20. 9 Cranch at 49, 3 L.Ed. at 652.

21. Ibid.

22. John F. Wilson, "Introduction," in Wilson and Drakeman, *Church and State*, p. 91. See also Ray Allen Billington, *The Protestant Crusade, 1800–1860: A Study of the Origins of the American Nation* (New York: Macmillan, 1938).

23. People v. Ruggles, 8 Johns. 290 (1811).

24. See Leonard W. Levy, *Blasphemy in Massachusetts* (New York: DaCapo Press, 1973).

25. Alvin W. Johnson, *The Legal Status of Church-State Relationships in the United States* (Minneapolis: University of Minnesota Press, 1934), p. 231.

26. Ex parte Newman, 9 Cal. 502 (1858).

27. The cases are found in section 154 of the *American Digest. Centennial Edition* 10, columns 1483–85. See also, Johnson, Alvin W., *The Legal Status of Church-State Relationships in the United States* (Minneapolis: University of Minnesota Press, 1934), chapter 16.

28. Johnson, *Legal Status*, p. 240.

29. Quoted in Ibid., p. 243. H. Frank Way has pointed out that "[b]etween 1817 and 1887, 25 percent of the recorded state Sunday closing cases offered a Christian nation or Christian piety rationale. Between 1888 and 1920 this percentage dropped to less than ten." H. Frank Way, "The Death of the Christian Nation: The Judiciary and Church-State Relations," *Journal of Church and State* 29, no. 3 (Autumn 1987), pp. 509–29, p. 517.

30. Ibid.

31. See Robert Michaelson, *Piety in the Public School* (New York: Macmillan, 1970), chapter 3.

32. Timothy L. Smith, "Protestant Schooling and American Nationality, 1800–1850," *Journal of American History* 53 (March 1967), pp. 679–95. See also Carl F. Kaestle, *Pillars of the Republic: Common Schools and American Society, 1780–1860* (New York: Hill and Wang, 1983).

33. See Raymond B. Culver, *Horace Mann and Religion in the Massachusetts Public Schools* (New Haven, Conn.: Yale University Press, 1929).

34. The Maine Case is Donahoe v. Richards, 38 Me. 379, 61 Am. Dec. 256 (1854), and the Massachusetts case is Spiller v. Woburn, 94 Mass. (12 Allen) 127 (1866).

35. Moore v. Monroe, 64 Iowa 367, 20 N.W. 475 (1884).

36. Weiss v. District Board of School District No. 8, 76 Wis. 177, 44 N.W. 967 (1890).

37. Robert Michaelsen, "Common School, Common Religion? A Case Study in Church-State Relations, Cincinnati, 1869–70," *Church History* 38 (1969). See also, Michaelsen, *Piety*, chapter 3.

38. Ibid., p. 202.

39. Ibid., p. 209.

40. Ibid., p. 211. Later in the century, another Ohio court concluded that a school board requirement mandating Bible reading in the public schools was constitutional and could not be enjoined by the courts. Nessle v. Hum (Com.Pl.) 1 Ohio N.P. 140.

41. Michaelsen, "Common School," p. 212.

42. Ibid., p. 213.

43. Ibid., p. 207.

44. Ibid., p. 214.

45. Ibid., p. 214–15.

46. Ibid., p. 215.

47. Ibid.

48. Samuel W. Brown, *The Secularization of American Education* (New York: Columbia University Press, 1912; reissued, New York: Russell and Russell, 1967), p. 120.

49. Ibid.

50. Michaelsen, *Piety*, p. 112.

51. Ibid., p. 168.

52. Ibid.

53. Johnson, *Legal Status*, p. 293.

54. Ibid., p. 31.

55. See Michaelsen, *Piety*, p. 170, and Robert F. Drinan, *Religion, the Courts and Public Policy* (New York: McGraw-Hill, 1963).

56. Johnson, *Legal Status*, p. 80.

57. See Leonard W. Levy's "Introduction" in his *The Fourteenth Amendment and the Bill of Rights: The Incorporation Theory* (New York: DaCapo Press, 1970), p. viii.

58. See Ibid. and materials cited in Rodney K. Smith, *Public Prayer and the Constitution* (Wilmington, Del.: Scholarly Resources, 1987), chapter 7. See also Edwin Meese III, "The Supreme Court of the United States: Bulwark of a Limited Constitution," *South Texas Law Review* 27 (Fall 1986), pp. 455–66, and Joseph M. Snee, "Religious Disestablishment and the Fourteenth Amendment," *Washington University Law Quarterly* 1954 (1954), pp. 371–407. Probably the most recent treatment of the issue is Michael Kent Curtis, *No State Shall Abridge: The Fourteenth Amendment and the Bill of Rights* (Durham, N.C.: Duke University Press, 1986).

59. Levy, *Fourteenth Amendment*, p. xvii. This volume reprints the Adamson case as well as Fairman's article that appeared in the *Stanford Law Review* in 1949, "Does the Fourteenth Amendment Incorporate the Bill of Rights: The Original Understanding."

60. Reproduced in Smith, *Public Prayer*, p. 263.

61. Ibid., pp. 263–64.

62. Richard P. McBrien, *Caesar's Coin: Religion and Politics in America* (New York: Macmillan, 1987), p. 82.

63. See the cases collected in Johnson, *Legal Status*, pp. 157–65, 191–96.

4

ESTABLISHING A NEW APPROACH

"The Lord gave the Word" proclaims the chorus in majestic unison during Handel's *Messiah*. (For constitutional purposes, we might say that the Founding Fathers gave the Word.) Following this simple declaration, the sopranos, altos, tenors, and basses trip over one another as the four voices warble up, down, and around the scales, singing, "Great Was the Company of the Preachers." Handel's playful poke at the clergy reverberates equally well in the constitutional arena, where judges, lawyers, and scholars have all raised their voices in the great church-state debate.

In constitutional interpretation, as in matters of interpretation generally, the choice of a particular interpretive framework necessarily affects the outcome. In the extreme, the interpreter can first select the desired result and then identify an interpretive framework to justify that result. This is the approach lawyers tend to take since their job is to obtain the best results for their clients. Scholars frequently try to take a more principled theory-over-practice approach in working towards comprehensive constitutional interpretive frameworks, although they too, I suspect, occasionally peek at results before solidifying their theories.[1] Judges have adopted a variety of approaches, and the first chapter's survey of establishment clause cases shows that the Supreme Court has sometimes tried to articulate a general theory of establishment clause interpretation (hence the three-part test) and at other times has clearly abandoned that theory in favor of a particular result, as in *Marsh v. Chambers*, the legislative chaplain case.[2]

No one could possibly endure a discussion of every approach to the Constitution in general or the establishment clause in particular, and I will not attempt such discussions here. We should, however, review the range of possibilities. At one end of the spectrum lies the proposition that we can interpret a Constitutional provision by reference to the text alone. The extent to which we use sources other than the text will determine how far we move along the spectrum until we reach the other end, where the text is seen as virtually meaningless or irrelevant despite the fact that an ostensibly "constitutional" decision is being made. As with most spectrums of theories, we are likely to find the most comfortable place somewhere between the extremes, although those who have set out to do constitutional interpretation either in theory or practice have established positions along virtually the whole expanse of possibilities.

A totally textual approach based solely upon the Constitution's words offers the promise of certainty, clarity, and consistency. This theory focuses directly on the text, arguing that we must confine our interpretation of the Constitution to the words immortalized in that document. We need only consult the "plain meaning" of the constitutional language, and we can discern the proper interpretation of the provision in question. We may need to consult historical sources to help us understand the meaning of those words as they were used when the Constitution's provisions were enacted, but we should not otherwise go outside the four corners of the Constitution.

Opponents of this text-based approach argue that a variety of historical, philosophical, and linguistic concerns compel us to bring external insights into the text of the Constitution. Without delving too deeply into these arguments, we can quickly eliminate narrow adherence to a strictly text-based interpretive method as the solution to our establishment clause inquiries. First, by making the establishment clause applicable to the states through the Fourteenth Amendment, the Supreme Court has already rewritten the word "Congress" to include not only state legislatures but essentially anyone acting under color of governmental authority from public school teachers to United States presidents.

Moreover, the word "law" now encompasses a wide array of state actions having little or nothing to do with the legislative bills that we commonly think of as laws. And most important, the heart of the clause, "respecting an establishment of religion," is irredeemably vague and susceptible to a plethora of interpretations. At no time during the last two centuries have the citizens of this nation shared a common understanding of the words "establishment of religion." The Supreme Court's almost hopelessly divided and often contradictory decisions in this area testify to the difficulty of grappling with these definitional issues.[3]

In fact, much of the interpretive confusion surrounding the establishment clause debates is rooted in the assumption of the combatants that the clause is ambiguous rather than vague. That is, people have assumed that "establishment of religion" meant one of two things to the Founding Fathers. It either meant any kind of governmental support or sponsorship for religion, as the strict separationists argue, or it meant preferential treatment for one particular religion, as the accommodationists assert. Faced with this "either-or" question, interpreters have generally proclaimed the evidence favorable to their desired results and discounted the rest. In carefully reviewing the First Amendment's history, however, we have seen that the accommodationist/strict separationist dichotomy has been falsely superimposed on the text and intent of the establishment clause. We are thus left with the task not of deciding which of two positions is correct but of deciding how to interpret the establishment clause among the wealth of possibilities, from a radically strict separation of church and state to an aggressively accommodationist position. Vagueness, not ambiguity, is the problem here.

If we then concur that the establishment clause is vague and not susceptible to a solely text-based interpretation, how do we select an appropriate interpretive framework? What external source or method is sufficiently compelling that we will use it to determine the content of the highest law of the land? Scholars in numerous disciplines have offered a variety of intellectually interesting solutions—or at least approaches—to this constitutional conundrum. They all share a common premise, one which our reflections on the establishment clause make compelling: that we must use some source outside the constitutional text itself to aid us in constitutional interpretation. The first, and perhaps most time-honored, approach is to appeal to the intent of the Founding Fathers. In its most narrow sense—in which we look solely at the words the "framers" (however we define that term) used in addressing a particular constitutional clause—this approach is little more than first cousin to a totally text-based approach; we are merely expanding the "text" to include certain statements of particular eighteenth-century men. As with the text-based approach, those statements may theoretically offer a readily ascertainable, clear, and compelling interpretive guide.

Former attorney general Edwin Meese has recently been the most vocal advocate of the use of the framers' intentions as the only legitimate source to consult outside of the sacred constitutional text itself, although others, such as judge Robert Bork and law professor Raoul Berger may be the best contemporary defenders of this theory. Meese has called for a "jurisprudence of original intention" which "seeks to discern the meaning of the text of the Constitution by understanding the intentions of those who framed, proposed and ratified it. The intentions of the framers supply us with our original principles."[4] Meese and others are particularly perturbed at judges who have, in their view, pursued particular political or social agendas at the expense of the framers' explicit intentions, thus creating an "unwritten Constitution" embodied in judicial precedent. As Raoul Berger has argued, in a modern constitutional appeal to *sola scriptura*,

> Why should "adherence to precedent" rise above effectuation of the framers' clearly expressed intention, which expresses the value choices of the sovereign people, not merely of judicial predecessors? . . .
>
> I assert the right to look at the Constitution itself, stripped of judicial encrustations, as the index of the constitutional law and to affirm that the Supreme Court has no authority to substitute an "unwritten Constitution" for the written Constitution the Founders gave us and the people ratified.[5]

This approach has been called a number of things, including "originalism," "interpretivism," and "strict constructionism." Each of these terms has acquired a substantial amount of both political and definitional baggage, all of which we would do well to avoid. I will use the word "originalism" for lack of a better term.

Almost everyone who has tried to interpret the establishment clause, including the Supreme Court, is an originalist of one sort or another and has assumed the authority of the founders' intent. Contemporary originalists in former attorney general Meese's camp claim that the historical record clearly shows that nonpreferential governmental aid to religion is not only constitutional but is, in fact, something the Founding Fathers heartily endorsed.[6] As a result, originalism has recently been associated with politically conservative values, despite the fact that appeals to the framers have been made by people wearing stripes of every color of the political rainbow. We should not forget that the concept of interpreting the establishment clause by reference to its original intent—going all the way back to the nineteenth-century *Reynolds* case—has cast the brightest light on James Madison and the Virginia struggle for disestablishment, all of which led to a strict separationist interpretation often favored nowadays by political liberals. In fact, until the most recent attempts to bring out the evidence for nonpreferentialist intentions that captured Justice Rehnquist's attention, the originalism debate has generally been won by the strict separationists who have succeeded in having the Supreme Court read "The Life and Times of James Madison" and even Thomas Jefferson into the establishment clause.

Neither the accommodationists who are currently calling for a nonpreferentialist original intent nor their strict separationist opponents have fundamentally changed the ground rules for establishment clause debate; each side has merely put forward the historical evidence supporting its position. Even Pulitzer Prize winning constitutional historian Leonard Levy has eschewed new theoretical constructions in favor of a twist on the originalism issue.[7] Seeking to counter Robert Cord and others trumpeting nonpreferentialist history, Levy has located a new source of strict separationist interpretation and inspiration, namely, the nature of the establishments existing in America in 1789. If these were nonpreferential establishments, his theory goes, then the First Amendment's ban on establishments must have been intended to prohibit nonpreferential establishments, the only establishments then in existence. The Supreme Court must, therefore, interpret the Constitution to ban nonpreferential as well as preferential establishments of religion. Thus, for Levy, as well as virtually all influential commentators on the establishment clause, the framer's intentions are both authoritative and sufficiently clear to mandate specific judicial interpretations in contemporary church-state cases.

Originalism has been attacked on a number of grounds. One of the more interesting arguments questions why the intentions of the Founding Fathers are any more authoritative than any other source of constitutional enlightenment, something usually assumed by the originalists. Terrence Sandalow, for example, has asserted that the framers' intentions should not govern modern constitutional interpretation.[8] H. Jefferson Powell has argued at length in the *Harvard Law Review* that the modern approach to original intent, which focuses on individual founding fathers, is not faithful to the hermeneutical approaches followed in late-eighteenth-century America, when original intent "referred to the 'intentions' of the sovereign parties to the constitutional compact [i.e., the states as political entities], as evidenced in the Constitution's language and discerned through structural methods of interpretation."[9]

We do not need to delve too deeply into either the theoretical or evidentiary elements of the original intent debate. Not only have we already discovered that there is no clear and convincing evidence as to what the Founding Fathers intended when they enacted the establishment clause, but we have also seen that there may well be no original intent at all. The record of congressional debates, ratification debates, commentary, and the like discloses a combination of disinterest and confusion about the meaning of the establishment clause on the part of virtually all the people we could conceivably call Founding Fathers. Their various "intents" can hardly be synthesized into a coherent, consistent mandate. Thus, while a doctrine of original intent might have some appeal in cases in which we can be absolutely certain as to the nature of the original intentions (assuming such a case exists), without that certainty such a doctrine becomes virtually useless as an authoritative interpretive framework. For each scintilla of doubt clouding the original intent issue, the utility of original intent decreases exponentially.

Now that we have abandoned the traditional, text-bound and original intent approaches to the establishment clause, we may feel uncomfortably cast adrift. Even Sandalow, no great friend of originalism, has noted that

> The view that constitutional interpretation involves primarily an elucidation of the general intentions of the framers is understandably attractive, perhaps not only

> because it seems to support the institutional arrangements we have established for giving contemporary meaning to the Constitution, but also because it is so comforting. The uneasiness, often the agony, and always the responsibility that accompany a difficult choice are softened by the belief that real choice does not exist. In law, the search for repose leads us to attribute responsibility for decisions to those who have gone before and, in constitutional law, to wise men we call "the framers."[10]

If we cannot count on either the text's words or the framers to interpret the Constitution, we must find someone or something that will. A number of erudite and thoughtful constitutional scholars have sought to fill in the gaps. This scholarly debate is hardly limited to the establishment clause. Rather, it revolves generally around the issue of "judicial review" which law professor Michael Perry has defined as "the practice of reviewing governmental action (or inaction) to see if it is, as it is claimed to be by the party challenging the action, unconstitutional."[11] And, as Perry and numerous other legal scholars have debated, the principal issue is whether judicial review should be "interpretive" or "noninterpretive." Perry defines interpretive review as ascertaining "the constitutionality of a given policy choice by reference to one of the value judgments of which the Constitution consists—that is, by reference to a value judgment embodied, though not necessarily explicitly, either in some particular provision of the text of the Constitution or in the overall structure of government ordained by the Constitution."[12]

Interpretive review, then, is closely akin to what we have so far called originalism. Alternatively, "noninterpretive" review is when the court "makes the determination of constitutionality by reference to a value judgment other than one constitutionalized by the framers."[13] This interpretive/noninterpretive dichotomy draws a sharp line down the middle of our spectrum of constitutional interpretation, dividing into separate camps those who find their answers in the Constitution and those who try to find a way to put the answers there.[14]

Noninterpretive review is generally seen by its detractors as "judicial activism," an epithet cast at those whose theories create rights not obvious on the face of the Constitution. On the other hand, interpretive review has been accused of being inherently conservative on individual rights issues, especially with respect to the rights of racial and ethnic minorities and women, since our forefathers were not always as progressive as many in the late twentieth century would like to be. To try to remedy this conservative tendency, modern scholars such as Ronald Dworkin have proposed an expansive reading of the Constitution.[15] According to Dworkin, the framers did not create a narrow set of specific constitutional guarantees, but rather incorporated within that fundamental text a broad group of values capable of spawning many individual rights not necessarily explicit in either the constitutional text or the framers' minds. Proper constitutional interpretation, suggests Dworkin, may well favor those broad values to the exclusion of the framers' specific intentions. Take, for example, a Constitutional Convention delegate who "votes for a clause guaranteeing equality of treatment, without regard to race, in matters touching people's fundamental interests," but who does not think that education is a "fundamental interest" and thus believes that racially segregated schools are constitutional. Dworkin distinguishes between the delegate's "abstract" intention—to prohibit discrimination in matters of fundamental interest—and his "concrete" intention—not to prohibit segregated schools.[16] Choosing either intention is fundamentally a political decision according to Dworkin, who posits that "no compelling argument has yet been produced . . . in favor of deferring to a delegate's more concrete intentions."[17]

Dworkin and others following his approach have been criticized for seizing upon values first and then reading them into the Constitution, thus leaving us no way to ascertain whether the values were, in fact, in the Constitution before they found them there. In other words, Dworkin is attacked as a noninterpretivist in interpretivist's garb. This criticism is, of course, even more pointed when we are urged to reach a decision based upon "abstract" intentions that contradict clear evidence of legislators' concrete intentions.

John Hart Ely, a professor at Stanford Law School, finds fault with Dworkin and others who have seized upon fundamental values that they read in (or into) the constitutional text because there is no way to say whether any particular values not explicitly found in the Constitution are more fundamental than any others.[18] Instead, Ely has advanced a theory of judicial review that seeks not to stray too far from traditional interpretive methods. He calls for judges to see that the Constitution does not establish a set of substantive rights or values but rather lays down the procedures by which the government must act. In countering the scholars who have relentlessly searched the Constitution for values, Ely asserts forcefully that "the selection and accommodation of substantive values is left almost entirely to the political process and instead the document is overwhelmingly concerned, on the one hand, with procedural fairness in the resolution of individual disputes (process writ small), and on the other, with what might capaciously be designated process writ large—with ensuring broad participation in the processes and distributions of government."[19] Ely goes on to focus on procedure, developing his "representation-reinforcing approach to judicial review" at considerable length, but we can stop here because Ely himself admits that a small handful of constitutional provisions, including the religion clauses of the First Amendment, do not fit his theory. While the establishment clause may have its roots in "fear of an undue influence," and therefore may perform "a structural or separation of powers function," the free exercise clause certainly involved "an important substantive value [the framers] wanted to put significantly beyond the reach of at least the federal government."[20] In fact, the religion clauses are part of "an odd assortment, the understandable products of particular historical circumstances—guns, religion, contract, and so on" and are thus outside the Constitution's dominant theme.[21] Ely therefore sets them aside, preferring to deal with the large number of constitutional provisions for which his representation-based approach makes more sense.

Ely has received considerable criticism from those who look for—and find—a host of values in the Constitution. These value-based approaches should certainly speak to the free exercise clause, which clearly involves a "fundamental" right, but they will have to be examined much more closely in regard to the establishment clause, where the "value" involved is difficult both to identify and to interpret. But the clause undoubtedly involves more than a separation of powers "process," as Ely suggests, since the powers being separated do not both reside within the government. Thus a court is not asked to determine procedurally whether a decision should properly be made by one branch of the government or another but whether a decision by the government is proper (either substantively or procedurally) in light of its relationship to religion. Unfortunately, Ely's innovative theory will not help us solve the establishment clause dilemma.

While both Dworkin and Ely assert that their approaches are rooted in the text and the framers' intent and are thus interpretivistic (although a far cry from our original originalists such as Meese, Bork, and Berger), Michael Perry, a law professor at Northwestern, has issued an unabashed defense of noninterpretivism in *The Constitution, the Courts and Human Rights*. He discounts those who seek to justify noninterpretive review by appeals to the Founding Fathers, such as Ely,[22] and others, such as Dworkin, who offer no compelling evidence to support their claims that the framers constitutionalized abstract concepts for history to define and redefine.[23] Then Perry takes on the originalists. He does this not by bludgeoning the orignalists' weakest position, but rather by employing a deft intellectual judo that appears to make originalism collapse by the force of its own momentum. He first admits that there "is no plausible textual or historical justification for constitutional policymaking by the judiciary" and that noninterpretive review "cannot be justified by reference to the text or to the intentions of the framers."[24] Then moving to his area of primary concern, human rights, Perry concedes yet another damning proposition: that the "framers of the fourteenth amendment apparently did not intend it to make applicable to the states the first amendment or any other provision of the Bill of Rights."[25] If these two points are granted, the originalists' conclusion that some decisions are an improper exercise of judicial policymaking follows naturally. But Perry is only setting up his maneuver, for if we concede these arguments, then "one cannot be an interpretivist—a consistent interpretivist, at any rate—and at the same time approve the

Court imposing *any* first amendment limitations on state action."[26] We must, therefore, condemn *Brown v. Board of Education*[27] and other decisions banning racial segregation, most modern free speech decisions, and a host of other Supreme Court cases that even staunch originalists such as Justice Rehnquist and Judge Bork have sought to defend. Noninterpretivism, therefore, is justified, in Perry's view, because it performs "the function of deciding what rights, beyond those specified by the framers, individuals should and shall have against government."[28] In other words, even the originalists do not want to live in the framers' world, so we must look outside the Constitution's text and the Founding Fathers' intentions to find the values we want the Supreme Court to constitutionalize.

Where shall we find those values that can, in Perry's words, "serve as a reservoir of decisional norms for human rights cases?"[29] He first rejects tradition, consensus, and other appeals to "fundamental presuppositions of our society," drawing on his archetypical originalist, Robert Bork, for support: "The [fundamental] presuppositions are likely, in practice, to turn out to be the highly debatable political positions of the intellectual classes. What kind of 'fundamental presupposition of our society' is it that cannot command a legislative majority?"[30]

If we cannot turn either to tradition or consensus, what will supply us with values so fundamental that we should give them constitutional status? Perry has identified a "particular conception of the American polity that seems to constitute a basic, irreducible feature of the American people's understanding of themselves. The conception can be described, for want of a better word, as religious."[31] Seizing upon the theme of an American civil religion first identified by sociologist Robert Bellah, Perry notes that Americans have always seen themselves as " 'chosen' in the biblical sense of that word; that is, they have understood themselves to be charged with a special responsibility, *an obligation*, among the nations of the world."[32] Central to this role of "chosen nation" is the component of prophecy, or what Perry says might now be called "moral leadership." And thus noninterpretive review in human rights cases functions "to call the American people—actually the government, the representatives of the people—to provisional judgment."[33] The point of noninterpretive review is to

> enable us, as a people, to keep faith with two of the most basic aspects of our collective self-understanding: our democratic understanding of ourselves as a people committed to policy making that is subject to control by electorally accountable persons, and our religious understanding of ourselves as a people committed to struggle incessantly to see beyond, and then to live beyond, the imperfections of whatever happens at the moment to be established moral conventions.[34]

For those who dissent from the Bellah/Perry conception of civil religion, Perry is willing to substitute for a religious vision a belief that there are "right answers—*discoverable* right answers—to fundamental political-moral problems."[35] And however we characterize the roots of those right answers, the courts are charged with the responsibility—and authority—to make those answers into constitutional rights of the people.

Perry anticipates the criticism of "moral skeptics" who claim that there is no basis in constitutional interpretation to favor one value over another. In response, he posits that "moral skepticism is a terribly difficult position to take seriously in this post-Holocaustal age" for there would be no way for the Supreme Court to "oppose duly enacted laws establishing segregation or abolishing freedom of expression or of religion."[36]

If we accept the notion that there are discoverable right answers in human rights cases, we must then ask where we should look for them. Perry is careful not to latch onto any particular theological or philosophical approach. Rather, he notes that "a right answer—that is, that racial segregation, apartheid, is wrong, or that state governments ought not to impose civil disabilities on non-Christians—frequently represents, in the United States, a point at which *a variety* of philosophical and religious systems of moral thought and belief converge."[37] We must, therefore, look to "point[s] of convergence among a variety of moral systems" to provide the content of our evolving constitutional values, thus creating a dialectical relationship between the "established conventions" manifested in electorally accountable policymaking and the prophetic stance taken by the judiciary that will lead to a self-critical and ultimately more mature political morality.[38]

Perry's thesis is certainly controversial, but it stands as a good example of a method of interpretation quite far along our spectrum away from a totally text-based approach. Even more interesting in our establishment clause context is the proposition that the courts should look to the convergence of philosophical *and religious* systems of moral thought and belief to determine the substance of constitutional law. But despite the intellectual appeal of the various schemes for a unitary approach to judicial review under the Constitution, these schemes have, if anything, only further confused our efforts to make sense of the establishment clause.

For example, David A. J. Richards of New York University's law school has argued that "political theory, wedded to a critical historiography" may be an excellent basis for constitutional interpretation, and he uses the religion clauses of the First Amendment as a "case study."[39] He proposes that "quite abstract philosophical inquiry" is appropriate, including

> a philosophical psychology of the relations among will, desires, belief, and knowledge, a naturalized epistemology of epistemic rationality, a theory of practical rationality and its connections to epistemic rationality, an analysis of conceptions of freedom, and an account of moral ideals of the person and the unity of the self. As a form of political and cultural history, the same account would clarify and be

clarified by the examination of deep metaphysical, epistemological, and moral shifts in Western thought.[40]

Quite abstract, indeed. And by its very abstraction, and the accompanying call for the Supreme Court to examine all of Western culture, clearly not the sort of thing the justices are likely to embrace.

Moreover, the Constitution cannot easily be shaped by a single-minded approach to constitutional law and theory. The Supreme Court has not adopted—and probably will not adopt—such an overarching framework. Each clause of the Constitution has undergone up to two centuries of definition and redefinition in the courts and in the lives of the American people. In working towards a useful interpretive approach for any one portion of the Constitution, we must meet it where it is. That is, we cannot ignore the unique history and problems associated with the establishment clause by trying to envelop it within a grand broad theory. We will, nevertheless, need to keep the tools developed by these constitutional theorists in mind as we try to deal with the words of the clause and decide whether we ought to invoke external referents, be they political theory or sociological phenomena, in the interpretive process.

Finally, we come to the sizeable group of commentators who have tried their hand at developing an approach to the establishment clause itself. Much of this literature falls into the seemingly ageless battle between the accommodationists and the strict separationists. As we saw in the earlier chapters, polemics dominate the field, although other less argumentative interpretive approaches abound as well, and there is no easy way to categorize the approaches, or to synthesize the best commentary into a coherent theory. Some scholars have taken the free exercise and establishment clauses and collapsed them into one theme. Scholar Philip Kurland, for example, has argued, "The freedom and separation clauses should be read as stating a single precept: that government cannot utilize religion as a standard for action or inaction because these clauses, read together as they should be, prohibit classification in terms of religion either to confer a benefit or to impose a burden."[41]

Lawrence Tribe, on the other hand, would take the word *religion*, which appears only once, and give it a different meaning, depending on whether the subject is free exercise or establishment. In a free exercise case, "all that is '*arguably religious*' should be considered religious," but "anything '*arguably non-religious*' should not be considered religious in applying the establishment clause."[42] Seeing voluntarism and separatism as the fundamental principles behind the religion clause, Tribe concludes that voluntarism is "more fundamental."[43] And thus, based on his review of the relevant history, "Whenever a free exercise claim conflicts with an absolute non-establishment theory, the support of the former would be more faithful to the consensus present at the time of the Constitutional Convention and of the First Congress."[44] Yet another commentator, who finds "strict neutrality" at the core of the religion clauses, asserts in the *Columbia Law Review* that "the free exercise clause [must] be subordinated to the establishment clause in every instance where the two doctrines are presently believed to conflict."[45]

Despite the plethora of scholarly attempts to aid the Supreme Court in establishment clause cases, no interpretive approach has supplanted the Court's devotion to the three-part *Lemon* test. Time and again, when a state action has been challenged on establishment clause grounds, the Court has applied the three-part *Lemon* test: "First, the statute must have a secular legislative purpose; second, its principal or primary effect must be one that neither advances nor inhibits religion, . . . finally, the statute must not foster 'an excessive government entanglement with religion.' "[46] Yet, as we saw in the first chapter, this test is laden with problems. Perhaps the most compelling criticism of the three-part test is the fact that it has failed to generate any clear or consistent First Amendment jurisprudence. Even the Supreme Court seems to be on the verge of abandoning it, although it is not clear whether its likely demise is attributable to flaws in the test itself or to a perception on the part of some justices that it has too often been used to support a strict separationist decision. Both are probably contributing factors, and although we must certainly acknowledge the force of the current justices' accommodationist leanings, it may be useful briefly to review some of the problems inherent in the three-part test.

The first prong of the test, the requirement that the law have a secular purpose, creates two problems. First, it has never been entirely clear whether the law must have exclusively secular purposes or merely enough of a secular purpose to convince a court that the legislators' motivation was not entirely religious. Second, an inquiry into the purpose behind a challenged state action raises the same kind of legislative history problems that we discussed in the second chapter. In fact, as Justice Scalia pointed out in *Aguillard*, these problems are magnified because we are not only asking how to determine a law's meaning but the purpose behind it. How can we ascertain the purpose behind a law (which may be very different from its meaning) when the law has been enacted by several hundred members of Congress, adopted by dozens of Senators, signed by the president, and enforced by hundreds and perhaps thousands of government employees? Even if all these relevant people were in total agreement about the law's *meaning* (an extraordinarily unlikely event), they are virtually certain to have a multitude of *purposes*. The Supreme Court's common practice of merely looking at the statements of legislators who debated the bill on the floor of the Congress, inevitably a tiny percentage of all of the lawmakers, seems unlikely to give an accurate picture of the meaning of a law much less the intent behind it.[47]

It is also unclear whether we are trying to ascertain the purpose of the law itself or the purpose of the legislators in enacting it, assuming we can distinguish between the two. Take, for example, the cases involving state laws mandating a moment of silence at the beginning of the public school day. A legislature could adopt a moment of silence law that does not use the word "religion" or any words such as "meditation" or "contemplation" that have religious overtones; rather, the law could simply provide for sixty seconds of silence at the beginning of homeroom. How should we determine the "purpose" prong of the three-part test under each of the following scenarios:

1. No one even remotely connected with the bill ever mentioned the concept of religion. The legislators heard many hours of expert testimony, all of which is preserved on the congressional record, from educators who lauded the moment of silence as a pedagogical tool.
2. The same facts as in paragraph 1, but the bill's sponsor has introduced two dozen prior bills, none of which passed, that would have provided for the public school day to open with a moment of prayer.
3. The legislators hear testimony not only from educational experts but from members of the clergy who support the bill because it will encourage prayer.
4. Some of the legislators state publicly that they are voting for the bill because it supports religion, others solely because it is good for education. The bill passes only by one vote, and the last remaining uncommitted legislator admits that she has no opinion whatsoever about the bill and voted for it solely because the governor promised to support an unrelated bill she is sponsoring. Does it matter whether the governor supported the bill for religious or educational reasons?

These examples should suffice to highlight some of the problems involved in determining the purpose of a law. The issues are even more complicated when a challenged state action is not a duly enacted law but instead an administrative action or a regulation promulgated by a state or local agency.

The inquiry into the second prong of the test, whether the law's principal or primary effect either advances or inhibits religion, is equally difficult. First, we need to think about why we are asking if the law might inhibit religion. That seems to be an appropriate inquiry in free exercise cases, but whatever the establishment clause means, it is probably safe to say that it relates to governmental support of religion rather than inhibition of it.

Second, it is hard to say exactly how to determine the "principal or primary effect" of any state action. Most people will probably assume that tax dollars flowing to religious institutions will have a primary effect of advancing religion, although there may be a sizeable number of skeptics who argue that most religious institutions do little if anything to further the cause of true religion. But it is substantially harder to gauge the religious effect of actions that may appear to benefit religion in a less tangible way.

How shall we judge whether a school prayer, moment of silence, the posting of the Ten Commandments in school classrooms, or even the teaching of the Genesis version of creation in lieu of Darwin's theory of evolution affects religion, and if so, whether such effect is the primary or principal effect of the governmental action? Is it fair to assume that the presence of an activity that is deemed religious by some people will, in fact, have the effect of advancing the religion of either those people or others not sharing their religious beliefs? Should we instead try to enlist sociologists to study church membership patterns or psychologists to interview public school students to ascertain whether the state action in question has advanced religion in some measurable way? As with the secular purpose test, these are difficult questions that may have led to the Court's insecurity about continuing the use of the three-part test.

The purpose and effect prongs of the three-part test share a substantial problem in that they require the Court to make a yes or no decision on these very complex issues. After reviewing whatever facts the Court sees as relevant, it must state that the law either has a secular purpose or not and that the law either has a primary effect that advances religion or not. The Court does not have the freedom to address the remarkably complex subjects of purpose or effect without making categorical black-and-white decisions.

Finally, we turn to the "excessive entanglement" test which appears, from time to time, to include a "political divisiveness" component. Of the three parts to the test, the entanglement prong is perhaps the most enigmatic. It is generally invoked in parochial school aid cases and seems to stand for the proposition that the government should not get its hands dirty (or clean?) by interacting with religious organizations. The Court has never provided us with any clear guidance as to when an entanglement between government and religion is sufficiently "excessive" to create an establishment clause problem, but it appears that any time state officials must watch over religious schools to ensure that state monies are not being used in furtherance of a religious purpose, there is an excessive entanglement.

The entanglement prong is thus the establishment clause's Catch–22. For decades, state legislatures have passed bills to appropriate funds for aid to parochial schools; these appropriations have been challenged by a vocal and litigious opposition that has brought many cases all the way to the Supreme Court. As early laws were struck down, the legislators added increasingly complicated schemes by which the state authorities would monitor and regulate the use of tax dollars in religious schools to demonstrate that the parochial school aid appropriations would benefit only the state's legitimate interest in education. Yet these very protections became the bills' principal constitutional infirmities because they created an excessive entanglement between governmental bodies and religious institutions. In other words, the harder the state works to make sure the parochial school aid bills do not have a religious effect, the more entangling the bills become.

Perhaps the best question to ask is, why are interactions between governmental and religious institutions a bad thing, or, if not bad per se, sufficient to render an otherwise proper legislative action unconstitutional? Religious institutions make up an integral part of American public life, and the government cannot and, in fact, does not ignore them. Religious schools, churches, and other institutions are organized under state laws and regulated by a host of governmental agencies, from those concerned with occupational health and safety to the Internal Revenue Service and state taxing authorities. Currently, a number of churches are petitioning the courts for relief from ordinances protecting historical landmarks that prevent the churches from changing the use or even the appearance of their buildings. It is hard to imagine that these kinds of regulations are less entangling than the unconstitutional entanglements found in parochial school aid cases.

The political divisiveness inquiry accentuates the idiosyncratic nature of the entanglement test. Apparently relying on Madison's "Federalist 10," the Court has occasionally suggested that to sanction parochial school aid bills would generate politically divisive legislative debate among warring religious factions. This proposition is remarkable, to say the least. Political divisiveness is a hallmark of American government. There was perhaps nothing more politically divisive in the history of the republic than the federal civil rights legislation of the 1960s, but the Court has let these bills stand even though many of the civil rights advocates, from the Reverend Dr. Martin Luther King to Lyndon Johnson, frequently relied on religious rhetoric in support of their cause.

As we saw in chapter 3, a long and bitter history is associated with the allegedly Protestant-dominated public school system and the Roman Catholic parochial schools that were formed as an alternative to the system. The factions fighting the parochial school aid battles have historically been divided along not only religious but also racial, class, and ethnic lines. The excessive entanglement test has, perhaps, been useful in enabling the Court to render judgments in these difficult cases, but virtually every commentator has pointed out that these decisions have been hopelessly inconsistent and confused. Unfortunately, the excessive entanglement prong is no better than its counterparts.

Thus, we need a new approach to the establishment clause. But in coming to this conclusion, we find ourselves in a dilemma. I have first argued that we must meet the establishment clause where it is and not attempt to erase the many decisions that make up its checkered history. Yet, at the same time, I am calling for a complete revamping of the approach we use to make decisions in establishment clause cases. To best resolve this dilemma, we need to develop an interpretive approach to the establishment clause that takes into account the relationship between church and state that has developed over the course of the last two centuries as well as the church-state themes that have emerged in establishment clause cases. Most important, however, we need a straightforward, workable approach that avoids some of the pitfalls we have observed in the current three-part test. Before attempting to formulate such a theory, we should briefly review the relationship of church and state in America and how the establishment clause has played such a fundamental role in shaping it.

By virtue of a number of factors—ranging from Supreme Court decisions to our country's modern penchant for litigation—the religion clauses of the First Amendment have become the vehicle by which our society organizes the relationship between church and state on local, state, and national levels. This need not have been so. The so-called battle between church and state could have been refereed by town meetings, state-wide elections, or national referenda. By giving the Supreme Court such vast interpretive power in *Marbury v. Madison*, we have allowed it to be the arbiter of federal church-state questions. More important, though, through the incorporation of the Bill of Rights into the "due process" clause of the Fourteenth Amendment the jurisdiction of the Supreme Court has become radically personalized, making the Court the regulator of state and even local church-state matters. The Court must therefore make church-state judgments about issues such as property tax credits for private schools or school Christmas pageants that were clearly not in the minds of anyone when the First Amendment was adopted. If someone had been prescient enough to think of them, the Founding Fathers almost assuredly would have said: "That's none of our business. We're here to put shackles on this new federal Congress, not to decide some local tax or schooling issue." In fact, we can view the current state of establishment clause jurisprudence as not only different but diametrically opposed to the intentions of the Founding Fathers. If we can say anything about "original intent," it is that the establishment clause was designed to ensure that religious establishments were not to be a *federal* issue. Whether or not we are convinced that the "*respecting* an establishment" language (echoing New Hampshire's "touching") was meant to protect state-established churches from Congressional intrusion, we must conclude from all the materials reviewed in chapter 2 that the members of the First Congress were ducking all important (i.e., state and local) church-state issues. Church-state controversies were abundant before and after 1789, but they did not surface in the United States Congress because they were not federal issues. Rather, they were confined to towns or, at most, states.[48] One of the most interesting ironies within constitutional jurisprudence is the fact that the Court's twentieth-century decisions declaring that the nineteenth-century Congress brought the Bill of Rights to bear on the states through the due process clause of the Fourteenth Amendment may have stood the eighteenth-century framers' decision on its head. Instead of being a local issue resolved by local governmental authorities, the most minute relationship between a church and a state has literally become a federal case and thus a national issue. Some have argued that matters of church and state should once again be made local issues and have asserted that the Supreme Court has improperly usurped state authority in these matters,[49] but, again, we must meet the clause where it lies today. Even Chief Justice Rehnquist would be loath to relinquish jurisdiction over state action in First Amendment matters.[50] And so, we must begin by wrenching the establishment clause out of its position as an eighteenth-century Federalist period piece, and give it meaning for the whole range of modern church-state issues.

This sounds as if we are abandoning both the text and its original meaning, leaving us to float aimlessly in search of a convenient interpretive perch. On the contrary, we must keep the text and the framers in mind in our effort to bring meaning to the establishment clause, but first we need to come to terms with the nature of church-state problems and why they seem so hard.

We need to acknowledge that the "church-state" rubric actually refers to a substantially broader set of relationships than this dichotomous term suggests. There is, of course, no single governmental "state" or unitary "church" in our pluralistic nation, but we can group a number of institutions under each heading. The "state" is divided into local, state, and federal bureaucracies, and the "church" is split into the many religious organizations dotting the American landscape. Yet we can still speak of two fundamentally distinct authorities, one deriving its power from the secular world, the other rooting its authority in the transcendant realm of the sacred. These two authorities inevitably interact with American culture because they compete to govern the lives of the American public.[51] Church and state—or perhaps more accurately religions and governments—occupy the same geographic location, their constituencies overlap, and they set norms by which millions live. Church-state controversy in the schools, then, should come as no surprise since that is where our children imbibe so much of American culture, from its language and literature to the often unspoken but vitally important values that communities share. Whenever important values are being taught, we are likely to find both "ruling authorities"—that is, religious and governmental—seeking to exert their influence. Because the two authorities are so deeply rooted in the American culture, it is culturally impossible to fully and completely separate church and state.

Many scholars have sought to define the religiosity that appears to lie near the heart of American culture. Perhaps one of the most well-known scholars is sociologist Robert Bellah. In 1967, his celebrated article "Civil Religion in America" identified a well-differentiated and institutionalized "civil religion" existing alongside of America's churches and synogogues.

Since then, dozens of scholars have brought a host of methodological approaches to bear on America's religious self-understanding and its institutional manifestations.[52] Although these scholars have failed to achieve any consensus as to the specific metes and bounds of the civil religion, the discussion has been useful in helping us focus on a broadly shared belief that America has a transcendent role in world history, or what Sacvan Bercovitz has called the "Biblical Basis of the American Myth."[53] The precise nature of that special role is unclear, but there is no question that in the minds of huge numbers of Americans, God and country are necessarily linked. And while the evidence for a civil religion is overwhelmingly based on Jewish and Christian images and traditions, it has a life clearly independent of any particular religious institution in America.

For the purposes of our establishment clause discussions, we need to recognize that vast numbers of Americans share a four-century-long commitment to a divine mission for America. No matter how strictly we might separate church from state, we will continue to find religion intertwined with the republic in the minds of at least a majority of American voters; a recent Gallup poll, for example, identified only ten percent of the electorate as nonreligious, and a clear majority favored school prayer.[54] For these millions of Americans, religion is in service of the nation, which is, in turn, in service of a religiously based higher calling. Accordingly, many of the activities challenged under the establishment clause—with the possible exception of parochial school aid—are designed not so much to benefit religion as to preserve the moral fabric and transcendent destiny of the country. Much of the outcry following the Court's banning of public school prayer and bible reading, for example, was centered on the ruling's damage to the country, not to the churches. Similarly, by singing "God Bless America," or reciting "one nation under God," we are affirming America's heritage and its glorious future far more than we are worshiping the Almighty.

Thus, the Supreme Court's enforcement of the establishment clause's strictures seems ironically unpatriotic because it threatens the religious underpinnings of our national self-esteem. This is not to say, of course, that we should shrink from strictly enforcing the establishment clause. But, in fleshing out the Constitution's mandates, we need to be sensitive to the forces underlying church-state controversies. Religious and governmental authorities continue to compete to provide order and meaning in American's lives, and the civil religious link between religious and national destiny further fuels the emotional and political fires inevitably raising the temperature of the church-state debate.

We can view the range of church-state problems as a spectrum that we can divide into three discrete segments. In the first segment, we can place cases in which there is allegedly an establishment of religion, and that establishment is not defended on the grounds that it is required to allow people freely to exercise their religions. We can call these "pure establishment cases." Perhaps the best example of a pure establishment case is *Marsh v. Chambers*, the Nebraska legislative chaplain case. A Protestant minister was paid with tax dollars to offer prayers at the beginning of legislative sessions. There was no claim, and could not be any reasonable claim, that the paid legislative chaplain was required for the free exercise of the legislators' religions. Moreover, there is little doubt that the activity itself, prayers rendered by an ordained member of the clergy, constituted "religion" (although we will need to return to the issue of how to identify actions as religious or nonreligious for establishment clause purposes). Thus, the legislative chaplain situation constitutes a pure establishment case. By affixing that label, however, we have not necessarily rendered a decision as to constitutionality. That will have to wait until we have fleshed out this interpretative theory a little further.

Along with legislative chaplain cases, I would include within the category of pure establishment cases at least the following: mandatory school prayers or Bible reading, imprinting coins with the motto "In God We Trust," posting the Ten Commandments in schools, and the reciting of "God bless this honorable Court" at the opening of Supreme Court sessions.

At the other end of the spectrum are the cases in which right to the free exercise of religion is claimed, with no concomitant establishment clause issue. These "pure free exercise cases" are similarly easy to identify. They involve a claim by people that the Constitution protects a certain activity from governmental prohibition or regulation. An example of the former is the use of peyote or other hallucinogenic materials as part of religious devotions, and the latter appears in statutes regulating church use on historic preservation grounds. Since we have focused on the establishment clause, we do not need to delve into the free exercise clause's complicated history, but we need to be aware of free exercise cases to enable us to best evaluate the middle segment of the church-state spectrum, the "mixed First Amendment cases," which involve competing establishment and free exercise concerns.

The mixed cases, which will inevitably be difficult, lie at the heart of the tension inherent within the First Amendment's religion clauses. There are times when the people demand free exercise rights that can only be satisfied by governmental involvement with religion. Perhaps the best examples are military and prison chaplains. These people minister to a literally captive audience that would otherwise not have the opportunity to worship in accordance with their faith under the guidance of an ordained member of the clergy. The service personnel and inmates, therefore, can make out a good free exercise case in favor of chaplains, yet for the chaplains to perform their duties (even if they are not paid by the government) they must be invited on government property and attend meetings scheduled by the governmental authorities specifically for religious devotions.

In assessing establishment clause cases, we need first to assign them to the pure establishment category or the mixed First Amendment category. Let us take, for example, the relatively easy case of a mandatory prayer at the beginning of the public school day that says "Dear God, please bless this school." This prayer takes place at a time when the teachers are in complete control of their students (at least in theory), thus eliminating a free exercise component (assuming that no student can reasonably claim that group prayer at that time of day is a religious requirement). It is well settled (and sensible) constitutional law that students surrender at least some of their rights during the instructional part of the school day to allow for the necessary elements of school discipline and authority. Once we have determined that this is a pure establishment case, we need to decide whether it involves an unconstitutional establishment of religion. We must therefore make two related inquiries. First, we must ask whether the activity is religious, and then we must decide whether the governmental activity is somehow an act "respecting an establishment" of religion.

The first inquiry—Is the activity religious?—is relatively straightforward in this case. The recitation is called a prayer, traditionally a word associated with things we consider religious; it addresses God, also a concept traditionally considered religious; and the language, such as "bless," also signifies an activity that we in America throughout our history have called religious. This is not to say, however, that the activity is, in fact, religious for all those participating. Nonbelievers who remain in the classroom may assert that they were not taking part in a religious activity, and even some of the most devout students may argue that the activity is not religious because it does not address Allah or is not undertaken at the proper time or under the proper conditions mandated by their religious faith.

While this school prayer would be considered "religious" by virtually any Supreme Court justice, we should note that the Court has typically taken the same approach to defining religion as it does pornography: It knows it when it sees it, but it cannot articulate a clear standard. Scholars, on the other hand, have written tomes on that very subject. To the extent that the Court has ventured into this debate, it has generally taken a theologically oriented view of religion, picking up theologian Paul Tillich's "ultimate concern" concept in some cases and deeming almost anything commonly associated with the traditional practices of Jews and Christians to be religious. In doing so, the Court has bypassed sociological or anthropological definitions of religion that focus more on the structure or function of an activity than its ideological background or content. Following Emile Durkheim, for one brief example, we might find a host of religious activities taking place at pep rallies and flag salutes, where theistic religion may be entirely absent. While it would be an interesting exercise to spin this approach out further, we need to remember that the Supreme Court seems to try to make its constitutional decisions generally comprehensible to the American public, a body that is probably not yet prepared to believe that high school athletic events are "religious" while prayers addressed to God are not.[55]

Ultimately, the Court will decide whether an activity is religious, and there is no way to provide clear guidance other than to suggest that the Court will undoubtedly continue to refer not only to the opinions of scholars but to what the broad spectrum of people in America have come to think of as religious. In doing so, the Court will probably ask whether the activity is one typically practiced by religious groups. This, of course, is circular since we call them religious groups because they engage in religious activities. While we could devote considerable attention to formulating a comprehensive definition of religion for the purposes of the establishment clause, it would end up being much too complicated to appeal to the courts. More likely than not, the justices will continue to know religion when they see it, thus most likely reflecting in their opinions a sense of what is religious shared by at least that part of the American public with similar educational, economic, and social backgrounds.

In evaluating what is religious in light of their current accommodationist leanings, the justices may be tempted to follow Tribe's suggestion that arguably nonreligious activities should not be considered religious for establishment clause purposes. In doing so, however, they should note that the accommodationist position is usually based on a desire to recognize and support the country's "Judeo-Christian heritage" (however that is defined), yet most things that would support that heritage would clearly be religious since the whole point is to support that kind of religion.[56] Accordingly, Laurence Tribe's approach may favor new or different activities, such as the teaching of secular humanism or transcendental meditation, that do not fall within out common conceptions of religion but may be in competition with or opposed to the so-called Judeo-Christian tradition the accommodationists wish to uphold. In most cases, either there will be little question whether the activity is religious or there will be good arguments on both sides of the issue. And since the difficult cases are generally idiosyncratic, the Court is likely to handle each individually rather than attempt to formulate generally applicable rules. We must simply hope that the justices address the issue of "religion" with care and sensitivity for the plurality of religious experience in America.

Once we have decided that an activity is religious, we come to the harder question of whether it is "respecting an establishment" of religion. Or, in other words, has the government done something unconstitutional under the establishment clause? Here, I propose we adopt Justice O'Connor's "endorsement" standard (without the accompanying "entanglement" test for the reasons discussed above). This frees us from trying to look into the minds of the legislators and also from trying to determine whether religion has somehow been advanced. Instead, we are asking whether the government has somehow endorsed religion. This does, however, create another definitional issue: What does "endorse" mean? Justice O'Connor has not discussed her proposal at length, but I would take it to mean providing some sort of tangible or intangible benefit to a religious activity or institution.

I propose that a religiously nonpreferential endorsement (i.e., a benefit available to all religions equally but not available to nonreligious activities) should be an "establishment of religion." The way to "accommodate" religion is by respecting the free exercise rights of the American people. If we acknowledge the wide range of religious activity in America, which includes not only Judaism and Christianity but Buddism, Hinduism, Islam, and a host of other religions as well, it is hard to imagine something sufficiently "nondenominational" to satisfy everyone. Probably no activities the government would choose to support are truly nonpreferential in such a diverse society. The traditional prayer at public events that mentions God but not Jesus may accommodate a substantial majority of Americans, but one of the primary purposes of the Bill of Rights is to protect the rights of minority groups (religious or otherwise) from the majority's ability to control the government. Similarly, we should not ignore the rights of nonreligious Americans under the establishment clause. Even genuinely nonpreferential aid to religion (assuming such a thing could be constructed) discriminates in favor of religious Americans at the expense of their nonreligious fellow citizens.

Fundamentally, I am asserting that the right to be religious is held by the American people and safeguarded by the free exercise clause, while at the same time that right is withheld from the government under the establishment clause. The government can, and indeed must, permit the variegated forms of religion practiced in America, but it may not act as the promoter or sponsor of religion. If we take this approach to the establishment clause, setting aside time for bible readings during public school classroom sessions is certainly an "endorsement" of religion as are ostensibly "nondenominational" school prayers. Leaving aside some of the parochial school aid cases, virtually all of the establishment clause cases in which state actions have been struck down would also be struck down under the endorsement test as would some (but not many) that have been upheld, such as the legislative chaplain case. Thus, we can offer the Court a method of analysis that will not require a radical break from precedent.

Although religiously nonpreferential activity constitutes an endorsement, I propose that benefits conferred to a broad range of charitable or educational institutions or activities should not be considered governmental endorsements of religion. Accordingly, police and fire protection for churches and tax exemptions for religious organizations that parallel benefits available to other charitable organizations are not endorsements and, therefore, establishments of religion.

This is certainly a controversial proposal, but it is consistent with an American culture in which religious institutions and activities continue to play a major role. We cannot expect the government to treat religion as if it does not exist or to withhold legitimate support for charitable and educational institutions solely because they have religious rather than secular foundations. The point of the establishment clause is to prohibit the government from giving religion special treatment; it should not be interpreted to single out religion as the one type of charitable organization ineligible for broadly available governmental benefits. By following this analysis, we can justify decisions such as *Walz v. Tax Commission* (which upheld tax exemptions for churches) without resorting to the Court's dubious "we've been doing it for two hundred years, and it has not hurt us yet" rationale.

The Court will inevitably need to decide how much evidence of a governmental endorsement of religion is necessary to create a constitutional breach. I propose that in pure establishment cases very little evidence of governmental endorsement should be enough to bring a verdict of unconstitutionality. In these cases, there is no issue of accommodating someone's religion; if there is a religious activity to be accommodated, then we are dealing with a mixed First Amendment case. Rather, the pure establishment case involves the government in putting the weight of either its name or its treasury behind some religious activity or institution. By doing so, it is discriminating against other religions to the extent that they do not receive the same benefit or in favor of religion as opposed to nonreligion. In pure establishment cases, then, I recommend that the Court adopt a strict separationist approach.

When we turn to mixed First Amendment cases, however, the Court should be free to exercise its accommodationist leanings (and should do so even if the justices were not so inclined). By definition, these cases involve an assertion by people that they want to exercise their religious rights and the government's accommodation is necessary for them to do so. In deciding mixed First Amendment cases, the Court should weigh the competing claims under the establishment and free exercise clauses against each other, and I propose that the justices put their collective thumbs on the side of free exercise. In other words, the free exercise claim should prevail unless the problem under the establishment clause is compelling. This approach recognizes and accommodates the religious faith and practices of American people without suggesting that the government has either the right or the obligation independently to foster our religious faith or heritage. If there is any one broad theme we can find in the establishment clause's history, it is (or at least should be) that the government should not be in the religion business.

There are no precise guidelines as to how the Court should weigh free exercise claims against the establishment clause problems, but the justices have applied balancing tests in other contexts, and should have no trouble adopting that approach here. Rather than attempting to describe such an approach in the abstract, it may be more useful for us to review a number of establishment clause cases to see how the Court might analyze and ultimately decide some of the controversies it is likely to hear in the next few years.

Equal Access Cases

Under the Court's traditional approach to the establishment clause, equal access cases present the classic mixed First Amendment dilemma. On the one hand, public school students argue that they have a free exercise (as well as free speech) right to meet for religious purposes during the time allotted for extracurricular activities at the schools. On the other hand, equal access opponents point out that there is a problem under the establishment clause if a public school opens its doors to religious activities. Although the Supreme Court has recently declared that the Equal Access Act is constitutional, the series of opinions in the *Mergens* case, none of which represented a majority of the Court, failed to establish a clear rationale under the establishment clause. It may therefore be useful to explore how equal access should be considered in light of the endorsement approach considered in this chapter.

In equal access cases, we must assume that the public school has allotted time during or after the instructional portion of the school day for extracurricular activities and that these activities are open to student-initiated groups as well as the typical school-sponsored programs such as competitive athletics. The free exercise argument is basically the following: Once the school has given the pupils the right to choose among a wide variety of extracurricular activities, and even to establish their own new clubs and programs, they have a right under the free exercise clause of the Constitution to engage in group prayers, bible readings, and other religious activities. To single out religion as the one activity inappropriate in the hallowed halls of the academy is to convey a strong message of governmental hostility to religion, a position long spurned by the Supreme Court.

Opponents to equal access argue under the establishment clause that any religious activities taking place during the school day on public property will involve governmental endorsement of religion and will have the effect of promoting or advancing religion. Moreover, public school students are young and impressionable and will be unduly influenced by seeing popular students taking part in religious activities. This influence will be exacerbated by the presence of a teacher in the room, especially if the teacher plays an active role in the religious activities.

This is clearly a case about which reasonable people may differ. Under the endorsement test spelled out above, however, the establishment clause problem goes away entirely if we accept the proposition that benefits conferred equally to religious and secular organizations do not run afoul of the Constitution. And so, while equal access is a mixed First Amendment case under traditional establishment clause analysis, it is a pure free exercise case in light of our definition of endorsement. As such, schools having open activity periods should be permitted not only to give equal access to religious activities, they should be required to do so.

Even if the Court were not comfortable holding that benefits may be conferred equally upon religious and nonreligious groups, I am convinced that the free exercise claims inherent in equal access cases outweigh the establishment clause problem. An equal access policy will either open the school to a full range of student activities, or it will permit most student activities with a limited number of exceptions. To single out religious activities as the only type of activity, or one of a few types of activities, prohibited by the school, strongly conveys a negative message about religion. For impressionable school children, placing religion on the forbidden list contains an undeniably hostile message that religion is either bad or is something the government would like to see disappear. Thus, the free exercise claims are quite strong in comparison to the relatively weak establishment clause problem (if one exists at all) created by giving religious groups the same benefits provided to all others.[57]

The issue of teacher supervision is a little more complicated. Simply having a teacher in the room to ensure the safety of the participants in the facilities provides little, if any, endorsement of religion if teachers play the same roles in the nonreligious activities. The level of endorsement will increase if the teachers are active participants, but they too should have a free exercise claim if teachers are permitted freely to participate in the other activities. Even with teacher participation, I am inclined to find equal access constitutional, and without teacher participation there should be little question that the students' free exercise claim should be recognized and upheld.[58]

Moment of Silence

There are several variations on the moment of silence theme. A number of state legislatures have adopted laws requiring that the instructional portion of the public school day begin with a short period of silence. Some of these statutes have specified that the time may be used for "prayer," "meditation," or "contemplation." In at least one case, the law reads that the students "shall be permitted" to observe a minute of silence, apparently to invoke the students' free exercise rights. As with equal access cases, the Supreme Court has avoided rendering a clear decision on moment of silence laws, although in *Wallace v. Jaffree* a majority of the justices suggested that they would support such a law under the right conditions.

Despite some attempts to invoke the free exercise clause, moment of silence laws are pure establishment cases. The silent period takes place during the instructional portion of the school day when the students are (at least in theory) under the complete control of their teachers. It is disingenuous, and even somewhat comical, to suggest that public school students are clamoring under the free exercise clause for a minute of peace and quiet while their teachers insist on noisy or distracting activities. As long as the activity takes place in the classroom during normal instructional time and students are not expressly forbidden to pray during silent periods, there is no free exercise issue.

So far, moment of silence laws have tended to run afoul of the purpose prong of the three-part test because the legislative history has made it clear that the laws' sponsors were seeking to use the moment of silence as an ill-disguised attempt to bring religious devotions back into the schools. Linking everything from teenage drug use and pregnancies to declining SAT scores directly to the Court's *Engel* and *Schempp* decisions, the legislators wish to return to the halcyon days when public education was firmly rooted in the Judeo-Christian heritage. With this kind of testimony on the record, the Court has found it hard to avoid the establishment clause problems.

As I discussed earlier, the purpose part of the *Lemon* test is flawed in a number of ways. Instead of using this test, we should ask whether a moment of silence law involves a governmental endorsement of religion. Absent any legislative suggestion about what the student should do during the moment of silence, the law merely mandates sixty seconds of quiet time at the beginning of school. While it may be dubious public policy for the state legislature to become involved in such a minute aspect of the public schools' instructional program, there would be no unconstitutional endorsement of religion. Silence by itself is respected by atheists and theists alike.

The legislative suggestion that students use the time for meditation, contemplation or prayer complicates the issue. The word "prayer" could be seen as an unconstitutional endorsement of religion if it is used alone, but not necessarily if it is accompanied by words like "meditation" or "contemplation" that have at least some secular usage. On balance, unless the law includes words that are strongly identified with religion, it should probably be held constitutional.

For all the reasons cited above, the legislative purpose or intent should not influence our decisions on pure establishment or mixed First Amendment cases. Accordingly, the "tainted" legislative history that has created problems in past moment of silence cases should not be considered in our analysis.[59] Similarly, we should not struggle to discern potential proreligious effects of a statute that appears constitutional on its face. We should, however, be aware that a constitutionally acceptable statute may create an unconstitutional endorsement of religion because of the way it is applied in specific cases. For example, a teacher who requires the students to fold their hands and bow their heads during the silent period, and then concludes with the word "amen," would certainly create an unconstitutional application of an otherwise constitutional law. We may, in fact, find it useful to analyze the constitutionality of a law on its face separately from our consideration of its application, and we can avoid the kind of speculation required by the Supreme Court's "primary effect" inquiries. Instead of guessing about a law's potential effect or assessing whether the religious effect is primary or principal, the courts can determine whether a specific application constitutes an unconstitutional endorsement. Our concern should not be whether a bill's sponsors proclaimed the power of prayer on the floor of the legislature but rather what the law itself does and how it is applied in real life.

Curriculum Issues

Curriculum issues in the public schools can be very complicated and emotionally charged; we can, however, start with an easy one. There is no establishment clause problem raised by public school teachers including historical, sociological, anthropological, or other studies of religion in their curriculum. The academic study of religion is no more an endorsement of religious faith than military history is an endorsement of warfare. Schools should be careful, though, to ensure that the academic study is not turned into a religious activity by a zealous teacher or a one-sided text.

A more difficult and recurring establishment clause issue involving public school curricula is whether the schools may (or must) teach the Genesis version of creation alongside or instead of Darwin's theory of evolution. It may be useful to separate this into two issues. First, there is the scientific question of whether the world was created in seven days or over an evolutionary period of several millennia. The second issue is whether God (or some other religious force) had a role in that creation. There is no question that the schools would be unconstitutionally endorsing religion if they taught (absent scientific evidence) that God created the earth, no matter how long it took to happen. Similarly, it would be unconstitutional for the schools to teach children about the origins of the human race by passing out Bibles and asking them to read from Genesis.

If we leave out the clearly religious component, the issues become a little murkier. The Court should first determine whether there is valid and reputable scientific opinion in opposition to Darwin's theory and in support of creationism. This is an issue of fact that the Court should be able to determine based on expert opinions. If creationism is scientifically supportable, then school systems and state legislatures should be free to decide whether it is an appropriate subject for study. If the Court determines that there is no valid scientific basis for creationism apart from its religious origins, then teaching creationism would be nothing more than teaching (and therefore "endorsing") a religious tenet in violation of the establishment clause.

This analysis has assumed that the creationism/evolution issue is a pure establishment case. Creationists could take the position that they have a free exercise right to have creationism taught in the schools. This right would be based on the claim that evolution is so inconsistent with their religious faith that the schools must teach creationism to counteract the potentially devastating effects of Darwin's theory on their children's beliefs. Again, the analysis should begin by addressing whether creationism is a valid scientific theory. If it is, there is no establishment problem if it is taught without reference to God's influence or religious texts. If it is not a valid scientific theory, then we need to use the mixed First Amendment analysis and weigh the establishment clause problem created by teaching a religious belief against the free exercise claim of the parents. I would argue that the establishment clause problem is compelling in this case since parents, by chosing to send their children to public schools, have generally relinquished control over the educational program to the school authorities. Those authorities are prohibited by the establishment clause from teaching theories based solely on religious faith, especially where parents have the option of private or home schooling to have their children educated in accordance with their religious faith.

Another complicated curriculum issue is the claim that current patterns of instruction in the public schools create an unconstitutional establishment of a "religion of secular humanism," in other words, a deification of human effort and potential thus creating a religious faith centered on people rather than God. Typically, religious groups (usually Evangelical Protestants) have wanted "equal time" to present the Christian alternative to secular humanism.

This issue is frequently treated less seriously than it should be. Too often, we assume that neutrality and objectivity will exist in the absence of religion, but this is not necessarily the case. The statements "God created the heavens and the earth" and "All people can live in peace and harmony if they try hard enough" are both affirmations of faith incapable of objective proof (at least at this time).[60] It is no more neutral to deny these statements than it is to affirm them, although there is probably more historical evidence supporting God's role in creation than there is showing that people can live together peacefully. While we can quickly spot the presence of traditional Judeo-Christian religiosity, it is harder for us to identify faith statements inherent in humanism.

This is not to say that the Supreme Court will (or should) declare the curriculum of thousands of public school systems to be an unconstitutional establishment of secular humanism. Quite to the contrary, the Court is extremely unlikely even to consider the matter seriously. The belief in human potential and numerous tenets commonly associated with humanism has deep roots in our culture and our civil religion. There is no way to make the public schools truly value free, and unless secular humanism begins to take on clearer institutional forms, it would be useless to urge the Court to see it as a serious threat under the establishment clause. In other words, while it makes considerable theoretical sense to see humanism in a religious context, we are struggling to develop a practical approach to the establishment clause that requires us to keep at least one eye on what judges and other Americans are likely to accept in constitutional decision-making.

Holiday Displays

What should the Court do about the crèche/menorah types of cases? The divided and acerbic opinions in *County of Allegheny* make clear only that the justices cannot agree on even the proper method of constitutional review let alone the appropriate decision in each different situation. Even religious groups do not know what they want. A case in point is *County of Allegheny*, where two Jewish groups offered opposing opinions on whether a menorah is a religious object and supported completely different outcomes in the case. If the American Jewish Committee and Chabad (representing the Lubavitch portion of the Jewish community) cannot reach agreement on the religious nature or message of the menorah, how can the Supreme Court be expected to do so?

Instead of following the Court's current direction—which appears to measure the visual impact of any arguably religious display in a context that may include numerous "secular" displays of reindeer, decorated evergreens, and the like—perhaps we should use the open public forum concept developed in equal access cases. If the County of Allegheny generally permitted the use of its courthouse steps for displays sponsored by not-for-profit institutions on a first-come first-served basis, nothing should be wrong with allowing religious groups to display their sacred objects. In this way, religion will not be unconstitutionally endorsed because it is merely afforded the same opportunity as every other charitable or educational organization. On the other hand, if the state property is not made widely available (and it need not be used, merely available) to other eleemosynary organizations, it should not be opened to religious groups solely because of the Christmas/Chanukah season.

Religion and Politics

After the election of John F. Kennedy, America's first Roman Catholic president, the issue of the proper relationship of religion and politics under the Constitution seemed to subside. More recently, however, with the rise of the Moral Majority and the presidential candidacies of the Reverends Jesse Jackson and Pat Robertson, this controversial issue has experienced rebirth. Religion has, of course, long been a part of the political landscape. As long as any religion in America sets its sights on bringing truth and justice to this world and not merely the hereafter, religion will remain a factor in politics. And, as we have seen through several centuries of American history, many of our most enduring and active religious organizations have long seen this land as the place we can—and must—bring about the Kingdom of God.

There are many elements of the religion and politics issue that are interesting to scholars and practitioners of both fields. Many of these discussions revolve around when a religious person should make a political decision for religious reasons.[61] Is it appropriate, for example, for a governor to veto a capital punishment bill because it is contrary to the Ten Commandments? Should it make a difference if the governor believes that capital punishment is wrong under moral principles not necessarily associated with traditional religious organizations, that is, what are often called "secular grounds"?

These are interesting questions, but we need to focus on the constitutional issue: Is it a violation of the establishment clause for religion to enter into political decision-making? Let me begin with the proposition that there is no such thing as "secular moral principles." This premise alone is a highly debatable statement, and for these discussions I prefer to use it as a premise rather than try to defend it as a conclusion. Whether or not this premise is defensible on philosophical grounds, historical and sociological evidence in support of it is overwhelming. There is simply no body of readily identifiable moral principles that is (1) not based on religion and (2) accepted as fundamental moral principles by all or virtually all Americans. In fact, the more controversial the political issue, the more likely it is that there is no religious or secular unanimity or even consensus about the proper decision.

My second premise is that politics and moral judgments are inseparable. Again, I defend this premise on sociological and historical grounds rather than theoretical ones. In addition to the manifestly morality-based issues, such as abortion or prostitution, many of our laws, from civil rights legislation to criminal penalties, are viewed by great numbers of Americans in terms of what is "good" or "just," concepts deeply imbedded in the American religious tradition. No matter how many ostensibly secular arguments may exist, the vast majority of Americans who deem themselves religious may well be influenced, probably to an indeterminate extent, by religiously based appeals. That religion and politics should be meshed at the level of the individual voter is a virtual certainty in practical terms, and the free exercise clause undoubtedly protects it in legal terms. We would be hard pressed to disallow an individual's vote because we perceived that it was religiously based.

Should we allow governmental representatives the same freedom? Certainly legislators should have the right to proclaim in open session that God favors one activity or another. Whether we believe them is open to question, but the combined forces of tradition and the First Amendment (free speech as well as free exercise) protect the right of our politicians to invoke the Almighty. In a representative democracy, our lawmakers must examine their reelection plans as well as their consciences whenever they vote, but there is no basis on which we can use the Constitution to eradicate religious rhetoric from the legislative chamber. And if we tried to do so, we would almost certainly discriminate against moral principles clearly aligned with common patterns of American religiosity and in favor of positions with roots in values that are equally religious but are not linked with the Judeo-Christian tradition.

Since we have eliminated the "purpose" inquiry from establishment clause consideration, we do not need to worry about whether religious motives will unconstitutionally taint an otherwise valid law. But is it right to allow the state and federal legislatures to enact laws that force nonbelievers to comply with religious morality? If we accept the premises that there are no truly secular moral principles upon which we all agree and that morality is necessarily a part of politics, then the answer is yes: Any time the law reflects a moral judgment, some people will be forced to comply with moral principles they do not espouse. There is no reason to discriminate against a legislative position because it is aligned with religious beliefs or because it is supported by a religious organization. Religious rhetoric and moral judgments are—and should be—inseparable from the democratic process in America, and the Constitution should not stand in their way.

Parochial School Aid

The current law on government aid to religious schools is a quagmire from which we cannot reasonably expect to extricate ourselves easily. Instead of trying to make sense of existing parochial school aid cases or to build a jurisprudence on that shaky foundation, we should probably abandon any pretense of following precedent and simply cnumerate a reasonable set of clear, consistent standards. Here is a range of possible results for future parochial school aid cases:

1. No educational aid other than fire, police, and other emergency protection may be provided by the government to any religious school or to any student who

attends a religious school. By electing religious education, parents are waiving any rights to share in governmental resources allocated to public education.

2. States may allow parochial school students to attend classes under the direction of public school teachers on public school property, but public employees may not perform their duties on the parochial school property. Likewise, parochial school students may use public school equipment and facilities when taking part in activities at the public school but may not take materials (other than items assigned to the students personally) back to the parochial schools.
3. Books and other materials used in public schools may be purchased by the state for use in all schools, either public or private. Likewise, bus services and other educational services (such as remedial reading teachers) may be shared by public and private schools even if the entire expense is borne by the government.
4. All aid to parochial schools is permissible, provided that parochial schools are treated on the same basis as all other private schools.

The reason these parochial school aid issues are so difficult is that any relationship between the government and religious schools can be seen as an unconstitutional endorsement of religion if we choose to focus on the fact that government goods or services are being provided for religiously based education. On the other hand, we could posit that the government's obligation to provide elementary and secondary school education is fundamentally no different than its obligation to provide police and fire protection to all citizens whether or not they are religious; in that case, the right to the best possible elementary and secondary education would be seen as more compelling than any establishment clause problems parochial school aid might cause.

Once again, the establishment clause can be interpreted to support any of these approaches, and the Court will have to use its best judgment. Under the endorsement test I have outlined, government aid to all private schools, whether or not they are religiously affiliated, should not create an unconstitutional establishment of religion (assuming that there are non-religious schools to share in the benefits). I believe that the government can make a strong case supporting the need for quality education, and that aid to private schools is an endorsement not of religion but of education itself. Since this is a particularly intense political issue, I would tend to defer to the legislature's judgment, especially since the constitutional provision is open to so many possible interpretations. Rather than invoke the dubious "political divisiveness" test that has surfaced in some parochial school aid cases, I would argue that such controversy is a hallmark of a pluralistic society and democratic government. There are many good arguments for and against aid to private schools, and they belong in the legislative chamber, not the courtroom.

CONCLUSION

I have set out to propose an approach to the establishment clause that will be clear and comprehensible enough to deal with the whole range of potential cases as well as consistent with the American tradition of church-state relationships. Perhaps the proposal's greatest strength is that it asks only one question to determine if there is an "establishment," that is, has the government endorsed religion? Endorsement may take the form of tangible benefits (such as money) or intangible benefits (such as prayers) made available to religious organizations or activities but not available in the same manner to nonreligious organizations or activities. Thus, if the government sponsors nondenominational prayer (even if it is bland enough to satisfy virtually all religious groups) it endorses religion but there is no endorsement if it offers tax exemptions to all charitable organizations (including churches) or provides subsidies to all private schools (including parochial ones). The establishment clause must be interpreted to bar the government from aiding religion in particular but must not be wielded as a club to discriminate against religion vis-à-vis other charitable causes.

By looking at church-state issues over the whole spectrum from pure free exercise to pure establishment cases, we should be able to encompass all potential establishment clause issues comprehensively. If there is an endorsement, we must inquire whether there is a competing free exercise right, thus creating a mixed First Amendment case in which we must balance the two clauses against each other. In finding a balance, the courts must review all the relevant facts and determine whether there is a sufficiently strong free exercise right to overcome the establishment clause problem. While there is nothing on the face of the Constitution to guide us in the appropriate form of a balancing test, I propose that free exercise claims be given the edge. Not only is there abundant historical evidence in the colonial and early national periods to show that the free exercise principle long antedated any broad-based support for disestablishment, but an establishment clause concern raised by merely accommodating some citizens' freely exercised religion seems far less dangerous to the republic than the pure establishment cases. Moreover, each time we side with the establishment clause in the mixed cases, we convey a message of hostility to the religion that may, in that case, not be freely exercised.

By viewing the religion clauses in this manner, we are recognizing two rights under the Constitution: First, that people have the right to exercise their religions freely, and second, that people have the right not to have the government establish religion. The first right runs deeply into the American culture, and it recognizes the continuing role religion and religious institutions play in contemporary American society. The second right, which ensures no religious establishment, cannot be interpreted as if the first does not exist or as if religion no longer plays an important cultural role. Our reading of the establishment clause must not be based on the pretense that religion is absent or that religious institutions do not, of necessity, regularly interact with both secular and governmental institutions.

I could, if pressed, invoke the acts and deeds of numerous Founding Fathers and other influential people in support of this approach. But that would be no more historically legitimate than the many appeals to the framers that we discussed earlier.[62] To be sure, this approach is as consistent with the Founding Fathers' intentions as any other, but that is not the point. Those wise men left us the task of figuring out what the religion clauses should mean, and we have no choice but to meet that challenge in the complex world in which we live. This work has been, I hope, a step in the right direction.

NOTES

1. Douglas Laycock, "Constitutional Theory Matters," 65 *Texas Law Review* 767–75 (1987), p. 771.
2. 463 U.S. 783 (1983).
3. Mark Tushnet, among others, has pointed out the difficulty if not impossibility of trying to interpret the Constitution solely in light of its text. Tushnet, "A Note on the Revival of Textualism in Constitutional Theory," 58 *University of Southern California Law Review* 683 (1985). (This issue of the *Southern California Law Review* contains a number of useful articles on constitutional interpretation, and will be referred to below as SCLR.) See also Michael Perry, *The Constitution, the Courts and Human Rights* (New Haven, Conn.: Yale University Press, 1982), p. 32. Perry notes that constitutional interpreters no longer expect the "plain meaning rule" to yield easy or conclusive approaches to the Constitution.
4. Edwin Meese III, "Supreme Court of the United States: Bulwark of a Limited Constitution," *South Texas Law Review* 27 (Fall 1986), p. 466.
5. Raoul Berger, *Government by Judiciary in the Transformation of the Fourteenth Amendment* (Cambridge, Mass.: Harvard University Press, 1977), quoted in Perry, *Constitution*, p. 68.
6. See, for example, Robert L. Cord, *Separation of Church and State: Historical Fact and Current Fiction* (New York: Oxford University Press, 1986).
7. Leonard Levy, *The Establishment Clause* (New York: Macmillan, 1986).
8. Terrence Sandalow, "Constitutional Interpretation," 79 *Michigan Law Review* 1033 (1981).
9. H. Jefferson Powell, "The Original Understanding of Original Intent," 98 *Harvard Law Review* 885–948 (1985).
10. Perry, *Constitution*, p. 76, quoting Sandalow.
11. Ibid., p. 6.
12. Ibid., p. 10.
13. Ibid., p. 11.
14. David C. Hoy, in "Interpreting the Law: Hermeneutical and Post-structuralist Perspectives," *SCLR*, describes Gadamer's approach to legal interpretation,

noting that Gadamer would not include noninterpretive review, as defined by Perry, as "interpretation" because of its radical disjunction from the text itself as well as from historical interpretations of the text (p. 139). Perry would probably counter that the courts are not doing pure interpretation but are engaging in judicial review, a process in which interpretation as Gadamer defines it may or may not play a part.

15. Ronald Dworkin, "Law as Interpretation," in W. Mitchell, ed., *The Politics of Interpretation* (Chicago: University of Chicago Press, 1983), pp. 249–270.

16. Ibid., p. 267.

17. Ibid., p. 268.

18. John Hart Ely, *A Theory of Judicial Review* (Cambridge, Mass.: Harvard University Press, 1980).

19. Ibid., p. 87.

20. Ibid., pp. 94–95.

21. Ibid.

22. Perry, *Constitution*, p. 21.

23. Ibid., pp. 70–71.

24. Ibid., p. 24.

25. Ibid., p. 16.

26. Ibid., p. 64.

27. Brown v. Board of Education, 347 U.S. 483 (1954).

28. Perry, *Constitution*, p. 93.

29. Ibid. Perry divides judicial review into three types of cases: human rights issues, federalism issues, and separation of powers issues (Ibid., p. 37). He concludes that noninterpretive review is proper only in human rights cases. Although he does not mention establishment clause cases, I will assume that they are fundamentally human rights cases (for reasons discussed at greater length later) and not separation of powers cases as Ely suggests. See Ely, *Theory*, pp. 94–95.

30. Quoted in Perry, *Constitution*, p. 94.

31. Ibid., p. 97.

32. Ibid.

33. Ibid., p. 99.

34. Ibid., p. 102.

35. Ibid.

36. Ibid., p. 105.

37. Ibid., p. 109.

38. Ibid., pp. 110, 112–15. Perry's intention is to develop a "normative" theory of judicial review that will create a functional model of constitutional decision-making. Because his theory runs so contrary to the democratic ideals our country holds so dear (by, for example, suggesting that legislative judgments be subject to final review by a Supreme Court that will be bound not by the words or intent of the Constitution but by their perception of what is on the cutting edge of religious and moral philosophy), it is extremely unlikely that the Court will adopt it as a normative theory. Yet, most observers of the Supreme Court's decisions would probably concur that many of its decisions are—in fact but not in theory—based precisely on the kinds of analysis Perry suggests. But instead of admitting that they are engaging in noninterpretive review, the justices work to find a way to give their

decisions the appearance of interpretive review. Thus, Perry's position is more normal than normative.

39. David A. J. Richards, "Interpretation and Historiography," *SCLR*, p. 530. For a fuller description of Richard's approach, see his *Toleration and the Constitution* (New York: Oxford University Press, 1986).

40. Richards, "Interpretation," p. 532.

41. Philip Kurland, *Religion and Law* (Chicago: University of Chicago Press, 1978), p. 112.

42. Laurence Tribe, *American Constitutional Law* (Westbury, N.Y.: Foundation Press, 1978), p. 828.

43. Ibid., p. 818.

44. Ibid., p. 819. See also Rodney K. Smith, *Public Prayer and the Constitution* (Wilmington, Del.: Scholarly Resources, 1987).

45. Steve Gey, "Rebuilding the Wall," 81 *Columbia Law Review* 1963, 1485 (November 1981).

46. Lemon v. Kurtzman, 403 U.S. 602, 612–13 (1971).

47. This analysis is complicated by the fact that many legislatures keep no records of floor debate.

48. Professor John F. Wilson has made the argument that the establishment clause was intentionally vague because the founders knew how divisive religious issues could be in the fragile new republic. See John F. Wilson, "Religion, Government, and Power in the New American Nation," in Mark A. Noll, ed., *Religion and American Politics: From the Colonial Period to the 1980s* (New York: Oxford University Press, 1990), pp. 77–91.

49. A few years ago, for example, Senator Jesse Helms spearheaded a drive to remove jurisdiction over school prayer cases from the Supreme Court. See S. 481, 97th Cong., 1st Sess. 1–2 (1981). Interestingly, Perry would apparently support this approach since he uses the possibility of jurisdiction-stripping as the method by which the people, through their elected representatives, can exert democratic authority over the Supreme Court's noninterpretive constitutional decisions. See Perry, *Constitution*, pp. 128–45.

50. We could, instead, follow some commentators and conclude that the Fourteenth Amendment did not—and should not be interpreted to—make the Bill of Rights binding on the states to the same extent as it is enforceable against the federal government. In fact, we saw in chapter 3 that the evidence supporting the doctrine of incorporation is weak and ultimately unpersuasive if we are to be guided by what we know of the intentions of the men serving in Congress when the Fourteenth Amendment was approved. Ultimately we need to set the incorporation issue aside as a red herring—not because the discussion lacks intellectual or legal merit but because the Supreme Court, as a practical matter, is extremely unlikely ever to renounce the power it seized over state action through incorporating the Bill of Rights in the Fourteenth Amendment. As Michael Perry has observed, to do so would turn the clock back not only on establishment clause cases but also on the far more important racial discrimination cases (e.g., Brown v. Board of Education). For better or worse—and original intentions notwithstanding—the states as well as Congress must live by the establishment clause's mandates.

51. This discussion of the church-state rubric is derived from John F. Wilson,

"Introduction," in John F. Wilson and Donald L. Drakeman, eds., *Church and State in American History* (Boston: Beacon Press, 1987), pp. ix–x.

52. Martin Marty has a good summary of these attempts in part 2 of his *Religion and Republic* (Boston: Beacon Press, 1987), and John Wilson has an important critique in *Public Religion in American Culture* (Philadelphia: Temple University Press, 1979).

53. Sacvan Bercovitch, "The Biblical Basis of the American Myth," in Giles Gunn, ed., *The Bible and American Letters* (Philadelphia: Fortress Press, 1983), pp. 219–29.

54. Norman Ornstein, Andrew Kohut, and Larry McCarthy, *The People, the Press and Politics* (Reading, Mass.: Addison-Wesley, 1988).

55. By this statement I do not mean to become further embroiled in the aspect of the judicial review debate dealing with whether the Supreme Court is, in fact, accountable to the American public in particular ways. Rather I merely assume that the Court would not *in practice* regularly issue decisions based on premises completely contrary to the common understanding of virtually all Americans. Or, if the Court does so, it is unlikely to be in church-state cases.

56. Going back to the legislative history debate, one could argue (following a line of reasoning paralleling Leonard Levy's) that the founding fathers were concerned only with the possibility of a Christian establishment since no other religious group could possibly have enlisted governmental support. Accordingly, there would be nothing unconstitutional in governmental establishment of non-Christian religions. So far, I have not seen anyone take this position, although it may functionally approach Tribe's proposal at least with respect to forms of religious behavior not viewed by the American public as typically a part of the Judeo-Christian tradition.

57. This analysis of equal access cases under the *Lemon* approach first appeared in Donald L. Drakeman and Robert P. Seawright, "God and Kids at School: Voluntary Religious Activities in the Public Schools," 14 *Cardozo Law Review* 252–84 (1984).

58. Under existing establishment clause theory, teacher supervision may be considered an "entanglement." Since there is no entanglement aspect of the First Amendment consideration theory described here, there is no need to consider whether teacher supervision creates an unconstitutional entanglement.

59. I took a contrary position in Donald L. Drakeman, "Prayer in the Schools: Is New Jersey's Moment of Silence Law Constitutional?" 35 *Rutgers Law Review* 341–59 (1983) because I limited my analysis to the *Lemon* test.

60. I do not mean to oversimplify the principles of humanism, secular or otherwise. I simply wish to point out that there are faith statements inherent in what we may otherwise see as nontheistic philosophies.

61. See, for example, Kent Greenawalt, *Religious Conviction and Political Choice* (New York: Oxford University Press, 1988) and Michael Perry, *Morality, Politics, and Law* (New York: Oxford University Press, 1988).

62. The combination of an essentially nonexistent legislative history and vague constitutional language has left us with no choice but to be noninterpretivistic in developing a functional approach to the establishment clause. This does not necessarily mean that we should assume that noninterpretive review is correct or even appropriate in cases under other clauses of the Constitution.

BIBLIOGRAPHY

INTRODUCTION

Cataloging all the books on church and state in America is a virtually impossible task. Recently, the Lilly Foundation sponsored an effort at Princeton University to create a bibliographical resource in this field, and the resulting multiyear effort by John F. Wilson and a corps of dedicated researchers yielded two volumes totalling almost 900 pages. This work, *Church and State in America* published by Greenwood Press, is indispensible for any serious study of these issues, and I will not try to duplicate either its breath of sources or its depth of insight. Rather, my goal is to point out and briefly comment on *some* of the influential and valuable works dealing with the establishment clause. In attempting to pare this effort down to a manageable size, I have either intentionally or inadvertently omitted many important books and articles. For these sins of omission, I will ask for the indulgence of the reader, and, perhaps more importantly, of the authors of those works.

SUPREME COURT CASES

The best-known collection of Supreme Court cases on church-state issues is probably *Towards Benevolent Neutrality* (1987), edited by Robert T. Miller and Ronald B. Flowers. A more recent entry is Robert Alley's *The*

Supreme Court on Church and State (1988). The relevant cases are also collected in abridged form in a number of casebooks, the most recent being John T. Noonan, Jr.'s *The Believer and the Powers That Are* (1987), which has a significant amount of useful commentary.

CONSTITUTIONAL HISTORY

Since the church-state controversies that we have addressed in this century as federal issues under the establishment clause were purely state and local issues in the eighteenth century, it is extremely important to appreciate the complexity and diversity of the relationship of religion to the various governing authorities during that period. The best and most comprehensive treatment of church-state issues leading up to the enactment of the Bill of Rights is Thomas John Curry's *The First Freedoms: Church and State in America to the Passage of the First Amendment* (1986). Useful source material on religion's interaction with government in the colonial period can also be found in William G. McLoughlin's *New England Dissent (1630–1833: The Baptists and the Separation of Church and State* (1971) and Mark DeWolfe Howe's *The Garden and the Wilderness: Religion and Government in American Constitutional History* (1965) as well as a number of studies that focus on individual states, such as John Webb Pratt, *Religion, Politics, and Divinity: The Church-State Theme in New York History* (1967); Jacob C. Meyer, *Church and State in Massachusetts* (1930); Susan Martha Reed, *Church and State in Massachusetts* (1914); M. Louise Greene, *Religious Liberty in Connecticut* (1905); Charles B. Kinney, *Church and State: The Struggle for Separation in New Hampshire, 1630–1900* (1955); Thomas E. Buckley, *Church and State in Revolutionary Virginia* (1977); and Sanford H. Cobb, *Rise of Religious Liberty (1902)*. A series of essays by leading scholars discussing Virginia's role is found in Merrill D. Peterson and Robert C. Vaughn, editors, *The Virginia Statute for Religious Freedom: Its Evolution and Consequences in American History* (1988).

THE FOUNDING FATHERS

The records of the First Congress, such as they are (and we must remember that James Madison called these records a "perversion"), are found in Joseph Gales and W. W. Seaton, editors, *The Debates and Proceedings in the Congress of the United States* (1834), usually referred to as the *Annals of Congress*, and *The Journal of the First Session of the Senate of the United States of America* (1789). A helpful resource for the ratification debates in the states is Jonathon Elliot, editor, *The Debates in the Several State Conventions on Adoption of the Federal Constitution* (1831) and Bernard Schwartz, *The Bill of Rights: A Documentary History* (1971).

Since James Madison and Thomas Jefferson have frequently been seen as the most important Founding Fathers with respect to the establishment clause, a significant body of literature has developed on their views on church and state in addition to the general literature on these American statesmen. For primary source material, see Julian Boyd, editor, *The Papers of Thomas Jefferson* (1950 and following) and William T. Hutchinson et al., editors, *The Papers of James Madison* (1962 and following). A handy compilation of the Madison materials on church and state is Robert Alley, editor, *James Madison on Religious Liberty* (1985).

THE ESTABLISHMENT CLAUSE

The amount of literature multiplies exponentially when we move to authors who seek to use the sparse constitutional history to support a particular interpretation of the establishment clause. Over time, Leo Pfeffer's strict separationist views of constitutional history as seen in *Church, State, and Freedom* (1967) and his many other writings have been extremely influential in the Supreme Court and scholarly literature. Carrying the banner for the nonpreferentialists is Robert L. Cord, whose *Separation of Church and State: Historical Fact and Current Fiction* (1982) has had considerable influence; parts of it have been read into the *Congressional Record*, and at least one federal judge has relied on it to ignore Supreme Court precedents. Between the Pfeffer-Cord endpoints, a number of interesting works lie along the spectrum. Leonard Levy's generally strict separationist work (notwithstanding his willingness to encourage "public support of everything secular in the private sectarian schools"), *The Establishment Clause: Religion and the First Amendment* (1986), is probably most important because Levy, a Pulitzer prize winning constitutional historian, wrote it. Philip B. Kurland's *Religion and the Law: Of Church and State and the Supreme Court* (1962) is a thoughtful work by a noted legal scholar, and a new volume by well-respected Judge Arlin Adams and Charles Emmerich, *A Nation Dedicated to Religious Liberty: The Constitutional Heritage of the Religious Clauses* (1990), which I have not yet seen, should also be influential. There are numerous other important works in this area, including Laurence Tribe's widely cited *American Constitutional Law* (1978) as well as the many other books and articles mentioned throughout the footnotes.

Additional information on these and other useful materials follows:

Alley, Robert S., ed. *James Madison: A Free Conscience in a Secular Republic*. New York: Prometheus Press, 1985.

Antieu, Chester James, A. T. Downey, and E. C. Roberts. *Freedom from Federal Establishment: Formation and History of the First Amendment Religion Clauses*. Milwaukee: Bruce, 1964.

Bellah, Robert. "Civil Religion in America." *Daedalus* 96 (Winter 1967): 1–27.

———. *The Broken Convenant: American Civil Religion in Time of Trial*. New York: Seabury Press, 1975.

Bercovitch, Sacvan. *The American Jeremiad*. Madison, Wis.: University of Wisconsin Press, 1978.

Berns, Walter F. *The First Amendment and the Future of American Democracy*. New York: Basic Books, 1976.

Beth, Loren P. *The American Theory of Church and State*. Gainesville, Fla.: University of Florida Press, 1958.

Billington, Ray Allen. *The Protestant Crusade, 1800–1860: A Study of the Origins of the American Nation*. New York: Macmillan, 1938.

Blanshard, Paul. *Religion and the Schools: The Great Controversy*. Boston: Beacon Press, 1963.

Boles, Donald E. *The Bible, Religion, and the Public Schools*. Ames, Iowa: State University Press, 1961.

Boyd, Julian P., ed. *The Papers of Thomas Jefferson*. Princeton, N.J.: Princeton University Press, 1950.

Bradley, Gerard. *Church-State Relationships in America*. Westport, Conn.: Greenwood Press, 1987.

Brant, Irving. *The Life of James Madison*. 4 vols. Indianapolis: Bobbs-Merrill, 1941–54.

———. "Madison: On Separation of Church and State." *William and Mary Quarterly* 3d ser., 8 (January 1951): 3–24.

Brown, Samuel W. *The Secularization of American Education*. New York: Columbia University Press, 1912.

Buckley, Thomas E. *Church and State in Revolutionary Virginia, 1776–1787*. Charlottesville, Va.: University Press of Virginia, 1977.

Cherry, Conrad, ed. *God's New Israel: Religious Interpretations of American Destiny*. Englewood Cliffs, N.J.: Prentice-Hall, 1971.

Cobb, Sanford. *The Rise of Religious Liberty in America*. New York: Macmillan, 1902.

Cord, Robert. *Separation of Church and State: Historical Fact and Current Fiction*. New York: Lambeth Press, 1982.

Corwin, E. S. "The Supreme Court as National School Board." *Law and Contemporary Problems* 14 (Winter 1949): 3–22.

Culver, Raymond B. *Horace Mann and Religion in the Massachusetts Public Schools*. New Haven, Conn.: Yale University Press, 1929.

Curry, Thomas John. *The First Freedoms: Church and State in America to the Passage of the First Amendment*. New York: Oxford University Press, 1986.

Curtis Michael Kent. *No State Shall Abridge: The Fourteenth Amendment and the Bill of Rights*. Durham, N.C.: Duke University Press, 1986.

Depauw, Linda Grant, ed. *Documentary History of the First Federal Congress of the United States of America*. Baltimore, Md.: Johns Hopkins University Press, 1977.

Dolbeare, Kenneth M., and Philip E. Hammond. *The School Prayer Decisions: From Court Policy to Local Practice*. Chicago: University of Chicago Press, 1971.

Douglas, Ann. *The Feminization of American Culture*. New York: Avon, 1977.

Douglas, William O. *The Bible and the Schools*. Boston: Little, Brown, 1966.

Drakeman, Donald L. "Religion and the Republic: James Madison and the First Amendment." *Journal of Church and State* 25 (Autumn 1983).

Drinan, Robert F. *Religion, the Courts and Public Policy*. New York: McGraw-Hill, 1963.

Dworkin, Ronald. "Law as Interpretation," in W. Mitchell, ed., *The Politics of Interpretation*. Chicago: University of Chicago Press, 1983, pp. 249–70.

Eckenrode, H. J. *Separation of Church and State in Virginia: A Study in the Development of the Revolution*. 1910. Reprint. New York: Da Capo Press, 1971.

Elliot, Jonathan, ed. *The Debates in the Several State Conventions on the Adoption of the Federal Constitution*. 5 vols. Washington, D.C. 1836.

Ely, John Hart. *Democracy and Distrust: A Theory of Judicial Review*. Cambridge, Mass.: Harvard University Press, 1980.

Fisher, Joseph A. "The Becker Amendment: A Constitutional Trojan Horse." *Journal of Church and State* 21 (Autumn 1969): 427–55.

Gales, Joseph, and W. W. Seaton, eds. *The Debates and Proceedings in the Congress of the United States, Compiled from Authentic Materials*. 42 vols. Washington, D.C. 1834–56.

Gaustad, Edwin Scott. "A Disestablished Society: Origins of the First Amendment." *Journal of Church and State* 11 (Autumn 1969): 409–25.

Gianella, Donald A., ed. *Religion and the Public Order No. 5*. Ithaca, N.Y.: Cornell University Press, 1969.

Greenawalt, Kent. *Religious Convictions and Political Choice*. New York: Oxford University Press, 1988.

Greene, M. Louise. *The Development of Religious Liberty in Connecticut*. 1905. Reprint. New York: Da Capo Press, 1970.

Handy, Robert T. *A Christian America: Protestant Hopes and Historical Realities*. New York: Oxford University Press, 1971.

———. "The Magna Charta of Religious Freedom in America." *Union Seminary Quarterly Review* 38 (1984): 301–17.

Hanley, Thomas O'Brien. *The American Revolution and Religion: Maryland, 1770–1800*. Washington, D.C.: Catholic University of America Press, 1971.

Hatch, Nathan O. *The Sacred Cause of Liberty: Republican Thought and the Millennium in Revolutionary New England*. New Haven, Conn.: Yale University Press, 1977.

Howe, Mark DeWolfe. *The Garden and the Wilderness: Religion and Government in American Constitutional History*. Chicago: University of Chicago Press, 1965.

Hunt, Galliard. "James Madison and Religious Liberty." *Annual Report of the American Historical Association for the Year 1901* 1 (1902): 163–71.

Hutchinson, William T., et al., eds. *The Papers of James Madison*. 13 vols. Chicago: University of Chicago Press, 1962–69.

Johnson, Alvin W. *The Legal Status of Church-State Relationships in the United States*. Minneapolis: University of Minnesota Press, 1934.

Johnson, Alvin W., and Frank H. Yost. *Separation of Church and State in the United States*. Minneapolis: University of Minnesota Press, 1948.

Kaestle, Carl F. *Pillars of the Republic: Common Schools and American Society, 1780–1860*. New York: Hill and Wang, 1983.

Katz, Wilber G. *Religion and American Constitutions*. Evanston, Ill.: Northwestern University Press, 1963.

Kauper, Paul G. *Religion and the Constitution*. Baton Rouge: Louisiana State University Press, 1964.

Kruse, Clifton. "The Historical Meaning and Judicial Construction of the Establishment of Religion Clause of the First Amendment." *Washburn Law Journal* 2 (Winter 1962): 65–144.

Kurland, Philip B. *Religion and the Law: Of Church and State and the Supreme Court*. Chicago: Aldine, 1962.

Kurland, Philip B., and Ralph Lerner, eds. *The Founders' Constitution*. 5 vols. Chicago: University of Chicago Press, 1987.

Larson, Edward J. *Trial and Error: The American Controversy over Creation and Evolution*. New York: Oxford University Press, 1985.

Laycock, Douglas. "Nonpreferential Aid to Religion: A False Claim about Original Intent." 27 *William and Mary Law Review* (1986): 875.

Lerner, Max. "The Constitution and the Court as Symbols." *Yale Law Journal* 46 (1937): 290.

Levinson, Sanford. *Constitutional Faith*. Princeton, N.J.: Princeton University Press, 1988.

Levy, Leonard W. "No Establishment of Religion: The Original Understanding," in Leonard W. Levy, ed., *Judgments: Essays on American Constitutional History*, 169–224. Chicago: Quadrangle Books, 1972.

———. *The Establishment Clause*. New York: Macmillan, 1986.

Littell, Franklin Hamlin. *From State Church to Pluralism: A Protestant Interpretation of Religion in American History*. New York: Macmillan, 1971.

McBrien, Richard P. *Caesar's Coin: Religion and Politics in America*. New York: Macmillan, 1987.

McClellan, James. *Joseph Story and the American Constitution: A Study in Political and Legal Thought*. Norman: University of Oklahoma Press, 1971.

McLoughlin, William G., ed. *Isaac Backus on Church, State and Calvinism, Pamphlets, 1754–1789*. Cambridge, Mass.: Harvard University Press, 1968.

———. *New England Dissent, 1630–1833: The Baptists and the Separation of Church and State*. 2 vols. Cambridge, Mass.: Harvard University Press, 1971.

Malbin, Michael J. *Religion and Politics: The Intentions of the Authors of the First Amendment*. Washington, D.C.: American Enterprise Institute, 1978.

Marty, Martin. "Living with Establishment and Disestablishment in Nineteenth-Century Anglo-America." *Journal of Church and State* 18 (Winter 1976): 61–77.

———. *Religion and Republic*. Boston: Beacon Press, 1987.

Mead, Sidney E. *The Lively Experiment: The Shaping of Christianity in America*. New York: Harper & Row, 1963.

———. "The Nation with the Soul of a Church." *Church History* 36 (September 1967): 262–83.

———. "Neither Church nor State: Reflections on James Madison's 'Line of Separation.' " *Journal of Church and State* 10 (Autumn 1968): 349–64.

Meyer, Jacob C. *Church and State in Massachusetts from 1740 to 1833: A Chapter in the Development of Individual Freedom*. Cleveland: Western Reserve University Press, 1930.

Michaelson, Robert. *Piety in the Public School: Trends and Issues in the Relationship between Religion and the Public Schools in the United States*. New York: Macmillan, 1970.

Miller, Perry. *Errand into the Wilderness*. Cambridge, Mass.: Harvard University Press, 1956.

Miller, Robert T., and Ronald B. Flowers, eds. *Towards Benevolent Neutrality*. Waco, Tex.: Baylor University Press, 1987.

Miller, William Lee. *The First Liberty: Religion and the American Republic*. New York: Knopf, 1986.

Morgan, Richard E. *The Supreme Court and Religion*. New York: Macmillan, 1972.

Murray, John Courtney. *We Hold These Truths: Catholic Reflections on the American Proposition*. Garden City, N.Y.: Doubleday, 1964.

Oaks, Dallin H., ed. *The Wall between Church and State*. Chicago: University of Chicago Press, 1963.

O'Neill, James M. *Religion and Education under the Constitution*. New York: Harper & Bros., 1949.

Perry, Michael. *The Constitution, the Courts and Human Rights*. New Haven, Conn.: Yale University Press, 1982.

Pfeffer, Leo. "Court, Constitution and Prayer." *Rutgers Law Review* 16 (Summer 1962): 735–52.

———. *Church, State and Freedom*. Boston: Beacon Press, 1967.

———. *God, Caesar and the Constitution: The Court as Referee of Church-State Confrontation*. Boston: Beacon Press, 1975.

Pratt, John Webb. *Religion, Politics, and Diversity: The Church-State Theme in New York History*. Ithaca, N.Y.: Cornell University Press, 1967.

Rice, Charles E. *The Supreme Court and Public Prayer: The Need for Restraint*. New York: Fordham University Press, 1964.

Richards, David A. J. *Toleration and the Constitution*. New York: Oxford University Press, 1986.

Richey, Russell E., and Donald G. Jones, eds. *American Civil Religion*. New York: Harper & Row, 1974.

Rossiter, Clinton, ed. *The Federalist Papers*. New York: New American Library, 1961.

Sanders, Thomas G. *Protestant Concepts of Church and State*. New York: Holt, Rinehart and Winston, 1964.

Schwartz, Bernard. *The Bill of Rights: A Documentary History*. New York: Aldine, 1971.

Singleton, Marvin K. "Colonial Virginia as First Amendment Matrix: Henry, Madison, and the Establishment Clause." *Journal of Church and State* 8 (Autumn 1966): 344–64.

Smith, Elwyn A., ed. *The Religion of the Republic*. Philadelphia: Fortress Press, 1972.

———. *Religious Liberty in the United States: The Development of Church-State Thought since the Revolutionary Era*. Philadelphia: Fortress Press, 1972.

Smith, Rodney K. *Public Prayer and the Constitution*. Wilmington, Del.: Scholarly Resources, 1987.

Sorauf, Frank. *The Wall of Separation: The Constitutional Politics of Church and State*. Princeton, N.J.: Princeton University Press, 1976.

Stedman, Murray S. *Religion and Politics in America*. New York: Harcourt Brace & World, 1964.

Stokes, Anson Phelps. *Church and State in the United States*. 3 vols. New York: Harper & Bros., 1950.

Stokes, Anson Phelps, and Leo Pfeffer. *Church and State in the United States*. rev. ed. New York: Harper & Row, 1964.

Storing, Herbert J., ed. *The Complete Anti-Federalist*. Chicago: University of Chicago Press, 1981.

Story, Joseph. *Commentaries on the Constitution of the United States*. 3 vols. Boston: Hillard, Gray, 1833.

Strout, Cushing. *The New Heavens and New Earth: Political Religion in America*. New York: Harper & Row, 1974.

Sutherland, Arthur. "Historians, Lawyers, and Establishment of Religion." *Religion and the Public Order* (1969): 27–50.

Tribe, Laurence. *American Constitutional Law*. Westbury, N.Y.: Foundation Press, 1978.

Tussman, Joseph, ed. *The Supreme Court on Church and State*. New York: Oxford Press, 1962.

Way, H. Frank. "The Death of the Christian Nation: The Judiciary and Church-State Relations." *Journal of Church and State* 29 (Autumn 1987): 509–29.

Wilson, John F. *Public Religion in American Culture*. Philadelphia: Temple University Press, 1979.

———, ed. *Church and State in America*. 2 vols. Westport, Conn.: Greenwood Press, 1987.

Wilson, John F., and Donald L. Drakeman, eds. *Church and State in American History*. Boston: Beacon Press, 1987.

Wood, James E., Jr., Robert T. Miller, and E. Bruce Thompson. *Church and State in Scripture, History and Constitutional Law*. Waco, Tex.: Baylor University Press, 1958.

Zollman, Carl. *American Civil Church Law*. New York: Columbia University Press, 1917.

INDEX

About the Author

DONALD L. DRAKEMAN is a Lecturer in the Department of Politics at Princeton University, and President of a biotechnology company. He holds a Ph.D. in American religious history from Princeton University and a J.D. from Columbia Law School. He specializes in religion and government issues and American constitutional law. Mr. Drakeman coedited *Church and State in American History: The Burden of Religious Pluralism* (1987) and has written articles for *Rutgers Law Review*, *Cardozo Law Review*, and *The Christian Century*.